Give Them
TRUTH

Give Them
TRUTH

TEACHING ETERNAL TRUTHS
TO YOUNG MINDS

Starr Meade

P&R PUBLISHING

P.O. BOX 817 • PHILLIPSBURG • NEW JERSEY 08865-0817

Unless otherwise indicated, Scripture quotations are from the ESV® Bible (*The Holy Bible, English Standard Version*®), copyright © 2001 by Crossway, a publishing ministry of Good News Publishers. Used by permission. All rights reserved.

Scripture quotations marked (NASB) are from the NEW AMERICAN STANDARD BIBLE®. Copyright © 1960, 1962, 1963, 1968, 1971, 1972, 1973, 1975, 1977, 1995 by The Lockman Foundation. Used by permission.

Italics within Scripture quotations indicate emphasis added.

ISBN: 978-1-62995-136-2 (pbk)
ISBN: 978-1-62995-137-9 (ePub)
ISBN: 978-1-62995-138-6 (Mobi)

Printed in the United States of America

Library of Congress Cataloging-in-Publication Data

Meade, Starr, 1956-
 Give them truth : teaching eternal truths to young minds / Starr Meade. -- 1st ed.
  pages cm
 Includes bibliographical references.
 ISBN 978-1-62995-136-2 (pbk.)
 1. Christian education of children. 2. Theology, Doctrinal. I. Title.
 BV1475.3.M43 2015
 268'.432--dc23
              2014047431

For Paul, long-suffering husband, enthusiastic fan, favorite friend, and still my sweetheart after all these years

Contents

Preface

"For who cannot see that thinking is prior to believing? For no one believes anything unless he has first thought that it is to be believed . . . everybody who believes, thinks—both thinks in believing, and believes in thinking."[1] —AUGUSTINE OF HIPPO

Pendulums swing. They never move from one extreme to the correct balance and then stop. Instead, in their quest for balance, they first swing from one extreme and then move all the way to the opposite extreme. This is just as true with ideas as it is with a physical pendulum. As Christian parents and teachers longing to pass Christianity on to our children, we understand that it is not the possession of information, no matter how much of it is possessed or how well it is known, that will make our children into godly, faithful followers of Christ. Our children must believe in and love the Lord Jesus. For many of us, that triggers a great sweep of the pendulum off to the opposite extreme, and we begin to neglect the *head* as much as we had feared to neglect the *heart*.

Our culture's attitude toward study and reflective thought only makes matters worse. In twenty-first-century America, the proverbial man on the street has little use for "academics" in any discipline. Such commitment to learning is for a gifted—or nerdy?—few who like that sort of thing. By and large, evangelicals in America hold the same cultural perspective when it comes to Christian truth. Who studies theology? Who reads commentaries? Who knows the Bible well—not just favorite psalms and New Testament passages, but the whole Bible? Pastors,

1. Augustine, *Basic Writings of Saint Augustine*, 2 vols., ed. Whitney J. Oates (Grand Rapids: Baker Book House, 1980, 1948), 1:780.

professors, and young men bound for seminary. Who else would need that much academic knowledge?

This book hopes to call those responsible for the Christian education of children to a fresh commitment to *educate children's minds*. I paused here to see how a dictionary would define *educate*, and I found the word defined as "to impart knowledge or skill." Another definition was "to train to be discriminative in taste or judgment." The intellect, or the *head*, is the subject of education, and it is to the head that I long to see Christian educators of the young address themselves anew.

Right up front, let me state loudly and clearly, so as not to be misunderstood, my recognition that imparting Bible knowledge and Christian truth to the mind is not all there is to Christian teaching and discipling. Not by a long shot! I do contend, however, that it is a starting place, and one so basic that there can be little sound discipling without it. I also contend that, in spite of its basic and essential nature, it is a starting place commonly neglected.

And perhaps this is so nowhere more than with children. For whatever reason (that swinging pendulum, I suppose), we view Christian teaching with a hands-off approach that we use with no other aspect of child rearing. We worry that if we teach Christian truth too much or too diligently, we will be "forcing" Christianity upon our children, and they will rebel against it. Yet with no such anxieties we require them to eat carrots and cucumbers (when they would prefer cookies and chips) and to go to bed on time. Requiring children to do what's good for them is simply part of being a parent or teacher.

When it comes to imparting a thorough familiarity with the riches of Christian doctrine or of in-depth Bible knowledge to children, most of us are surprisingly laid-back. We make sure children attend church and perhaps a children's class once a week, and we read them a Bible story every now and then, and we seem to think they will get the rest of what they need on their own. The foolishness of such an approach becomes apparent when we imagine teaching reading or math in so haphazard a way. We insist that children study those subjects daily. We make sure that capable teachers follow a plan for increasing children's knowledge incrementally. We require children to drill and to exercise their new skills on a regular basis. Why do we think that learning the most profound content that exists does not require similar diligence? Why do we think that the knowledge essential for living life to the fullest, knowledge that is, in fact, a matter of life and death itself, deserves less of a commitment of time and energy?

This is not a book on parenting. It is a book on teaching, and it is directed to anyone—parent, grandparent, teacher, or pastor—who teaches children. I have been teaching children and teenagers for three decades (wow! how did *that* happen?). My teaching has been in churches, in Christian schools, and in my living room with homeschooled children. So I work exclusively with children whose families identify themselves as Christians and who attend Protestant churches. While I am delighted that many of my students' parents provide diligent, consistent instruction in Bible and doctrine (sometimes better than what I provided for my own children), the majority of my students come to me with appalling ignorance of the Bible and its teaching.

My hope in writing this book is to expose that appalling ignorance to those who are in a position to do something about it. The book is in three parts. Part One makes my case: too many children from Christian homes do not know their Bibles and do not grasp Christian doctrine. Yet the possession of such knowledge is essential for everything else we desire for the spiritual lives of children. We will help prepare our children for every trial they will face as they live in a fallen world when we give them a firm understanding of the Bible and the teaching it provides.

Part Two showcases basic Christian doctrines children should grow up learning, providing some hints on ways we can communicate these things to our children and pointing out some of the clashes that occur between these teachings and the ideas of the culture our children will inhabit. Part Three details some specifics for teaching our children: first, general principles, then specific Bible content, and finally, doctrinal truths. As an acknowledgment that there is more to the Christian training of children than simply imparting information, the book concludes with a list of added resources. Some of the resources will help with the studying and teaching that is urged in this book; other resources will help with additional aspects of raising children so that we point them to Christ as they grow.

My hope in writing this book is to call parents, teachers, and churches to the Christian education of children's minds as a means to an end. I hope to remind Christian educators of all kinds of the importance of a most basic foundation. I want to encourage them to impart knowledge, facts, and truth to children's heads *first*, in order to give their hearts something to love and to live by.

Acknowledgments

This book would never have happened if it were just up to me and my laptop.

Thank you to Ian Thompson and the folks at P&R for being willing to see this project get into print.

Special thanks to Julia Craig, Jim Holmes, and Amanda Martin, exceptional editors who make me look much better than I am.

Much appreciation goes to agent Steve Laube, who, so far, has never been too busy to answer me promptly and who is helpful on so many levels.

Thank you, Patti Sanger and the gracious guinea pigs at Knox PCA in Harrison Township, Michigan, for letting me test the material on you one Saturday morning last October.

And, as always, thank you to my dear sweet love who has cheerfully gone off to work every day for years so I can be free to write.

PART ONE

Why Our Children
Need to Know

1

Head First: Truth Is
for Knowing

She had longed for this all her life. She had never had a name for it, but the desire had hovered in the back of her heart when she was busy, and had burst forth demanding attention when she had the time to stop and notice. She lived a comfortable life, was a member of a family that loved her, and had no complaints. Yet nothing ever satisfied. She had always longed for something more without being able to identify exactly what. Now she knew. All the dry places in her soul soaked up, with glad greediness, the words that rained around her. And still she thirsted. "I will never have enough," she thought, looking up into the face of the speaker from her cushion on the floor. "I will always want more, and more, and more."

"Lord!" Mary jumped at the harsh voice from the doorway. She looked up and saw a woman with a stack of serving dishes in her hands, her hair coming loose from under her head covering and her face glowing with perspiration. Mary knew what would come next. She felt a guilty flush rise up her neck and cover her face. "Do you not care that my sister has left me to serve alone? Tell her then to help me," demanded the woman in the doorway.

Mary prepared to scramble to her feet, but sank back onto her cushion at the sound of Jesus' voice, gentle, yet scolding, and addressed, not to her, but to Martha. "Martha, Martha," Jesus said, "you are anxious and troubled about many things, but one thing is necessary. Mary has chosen the good portion which will not be taken away from her."[1]

1. See Luke 10:38–42.

He handled pearls as other people handled small change. He knew their value—who better?—yet, for him, they were the stuff of his ordinary, workaday world. He had dealt in pearls all his life. He could tell at a glance which ones were a waste of his time, fit only for purchase by a farmer needing to appease an offended wife. This merchant sought out perfect pearls, the roundest, the ones of greatest luster. The dealers in pearls would see him coming and pull out only their best for him, and, still, he purchased very few of all he saw.

This pearl, however, had forced all the air from his lungs and replaced it with a sharp ache in his chest and his throat. *Could there really be a pearl such as this?* It glowed sweetly among the other pearls on the table, and they were little clods of dirt by comparison. The merchant picked up the pearl with careful fingers, placed it in the palm of his other hand, and lifted it up near his face. It was larger than most pearls, and the closest thing to perfect roundness the merchant had ever seen. All pearls had their imperfections; the trick was in finding pearls with such slight imperfections that a buyer would not notice them. The merchant could not see a single fault in this pearl. All he saw was his own face, reflected, tiny but clear, on the pearl's surface. He set the pearl down, and remembered to breathe. "How much?" he croaked. "How much for the pearl?"

When the answer came back, the merchant did not hesitate. He drew the bag of gold from inside his cloak and held it out. It contained his whole allotment for purchasing pearls for the rest of the year. "Take this," he ordered, "and hold the pearl for me. I will be back with the rest." The merchant hurried out the door, on his way to sell everything he owned so he could buy the pearl of great value.[2]

Who respected him now? That excellent education he had acquired, where he had always been at the top of his class, no longer meant a thing to all who had been so impressed before. The rising star he had ridden,

2. See Matt. 13:45.

both in scholarly and in religious circles, had gone down in flames. He sat, imprisoned, writing a letter to friends far away. Time dragged on—a year, two, several—while he waited for a trial and wondered what would happen. Would he be set free? Or would he be put to death? He had committed no crime, yet plenty of people longed to see him dead. The prisoner picked up the pen and wrote, "But whatever gain I had, I counted as loss for the sake of Christ. Indeed, I count everything as loss because of the surpassing value of knowing Christ Jesus my Lord."[3]

We would all like to see our daughters in Mary's seat at Jesus' feet, choosing the one thing necessary. We would all wish for our sons to give all they have with joy in exchange for laying hold of the kingdom of God, as the merchant did for the pearl of great value. The heart's desire of every Sunday school teacher or teacher of Bible in a Christian school is that their students, like Paul, would count everything else as rubbish for the sake of knowing Christ.

In order for our children to choose the one thing necessary, to supremely value Christ and his kingdom above all else, there are things they must *know*, and that is the reason for this book. *Knowing*—holding truths in our minds with which we are well acquainted and of which we are certain—has taken quite a hit in Christian circles in the last generation or two. We want to *experience* our Christianity; we want to *feel* our Christianity; we want to *demonstrate* our Christianity with acts of love and service. But knowing things, filling our minds with content, has come to seem less than spiritual. And so, without realizing it, we often neglect the very foundation of all that we desire for our children.

WHY THIS BOOK?

"Whatever else they don't have, the most important thing is that my children have their own relationship with God."

3. See Phil. 3:7–8.

"The goal of my teaching is for my children to consistently apply the Word of God to their lives."

"What I hope to pass on to my children is a heart for the kingdom of God. I want them to have a passion for Christian mission and service."

"I want my children to embrace the gospel for themselves and to share it with others."

"It's very simple; I want my children to love Jesus. I want them to live for him, seeking him and serving him."

The desires in that list make valid, worthwhile goals. Reaching these goals, however, requires a multileveled foundation. In my experience, most of the time, the bottom level—the foundation for every one of the goals listed above—is neglected, sometimes even deliberately rejected.

Knowledge—facts, doctrines, propositional truth, redemptive history, *head knowledge*, if you will—provides the basic foundation for every desirable goal in that list. Mary's choice, Paul's values, and the pearl merchant's hunger all presuppose a measure of understanding. Yet in my experience, "Christian education" for children often falls into one of two categories: it either neglects methodical, diligent instruction in Bible and doctrine, or it deliberately shuns it.

In my three decades of teaching children and teens, I have worked almost exclusively with children of Christian parents, parents who have a church they attend and love, parents (usually) who have chosen Christian school or homeschool for their children precisely because they want them to grow up knowing and loving Christ. These parents assume their children are getting all they need from their churches, their youth programs, their parents' example and teaching. Yet I find, increasingly as the years go by, that the children and teens I teach know only the most common stories from the Bible—and they don't know those very well. Their ideas of basic Christian doctrine are even weaker. My experience is that parents think they are raising their children in the nurture and admonition of the Lord while, in reality, their children (who are usually well-behaved and polite) possess very little understanding of the faith they supposedly embrace. One honest homeschool mom I know sees the problem and gives this analysis of the reason: "There are so many areas in which it's important to keep up—math, science, language arts; we can't let our kids get behind. Then there are the sports and the music lessons and practice for both. When we run out of time, it's easy to think, 'We'll get to Bible later.' But then, we don't."

Please understand that when I advocate Christian education for children, I mean more than church attendance, involvement in youth group, prayer before meals, and occasional home Bible stories or devotions. What our children need and, for the most part, are not receiving, is systematic, intentional—dare I say it, even rigorous?—instruction in Bible and in Christian doctrine, instruction provided as though these were subjects we expected our children to master. I'm calling for children to know the overall organization of the whole Bible, the big picture of the history it recounts, at least the important stories of all its main characters, and how the people and places and events of one Bible era relate to those of other eras. I want them to have a comfortable familiarity with basic Bible themes and to know definitions for concepts that are critical in understanding Christian doctrine. I desire to see them growing steadily in their ability to articulate these things.

Nothing in the universe challenges the mind like the consideration of the person of God. Knowing God involves far more than merely knowing *about* him; still, it certainly begins there. God has given us a whole book—a fairly long, fairly dense book at that. Surely he intended for us to know what it contains. The truths of Christianity and of salvation in particular number among the most complex, deep ideas humans have ever considered. To master content as rich and substantive as that which God has given—and we do want to master it, don't we, if God has given it?—requires diligent study and work. Why would we think our children will know God and understand the doctrines of Scripture if we have not deliberately, diligently, consistently taught the truths God has revealed? An occasional reading from a Bible storybook, a quick prayer before dinner or at bedtime, and regular trips to church do not supply all the Christian education children need.

I have met well-intentioned parents and teachers who neglect rigorous teaching for children on purpose. They fear that in-depth Bible teaching, memorization, and doctrinal instruction will turn into "head knowledge" for children, something to avoid because of how it might work against what we really want for them.

"We're not interested in giving kids mere head knowledge," I hear. "We're looking for application. Christianity needs to be from the heart." *Of course* learning information is not enough. An intellectual awareness of all the right things does not equal biblical Christianity. *Of course* the ultimate goal is applying Scripture, loving Christ, and obeying God from the heart. But too many times when parents have told me they don't want "*just* head knowledge," they've made it clear that they really don't want head knowledge at all; they want something else instead. They want character lessons and moral maxims their children can apply immediately. They want experiences for their children that will result in positive feelings about Jesus now. Many adults seem to believe that, if we teach Bible diligently and purposefully, at best, we will bore children. At worst, they think, such teaching will make children proud of what they know, resulting in hardened, self-righteous hearts.

But consider how basic a correct, intellectual knowledge is to all those admirable goals listed earlier.

"Whatever else they don't have, the most important thing is that my children have their own relationship with God." True, but what God do we mean? There are almost as many ideas of who God is as there are persons to have those ideas, and what most Westerners have come to mean by "God" does not resemble at all the God who has revealed himself in Scripture. How will your child know the difference between people's *ideas* of God—including his or her own ideas—and the true God, who has revealed himself in his Word? Many religions, pseudo-religions, and cults offer a way to what they call "God." All those paths cannot be right. How will your child know whom to listen to and whom to ignore when people promise her "God"? God is so *other* than we are that we can never arrive at knowing what he's like on our own. With amazing concision, God packed all we need to know about him into one book—but it is *one whole book*, after all.

It required centuries for God to reveal, in the written Scriptures, all he wanted known about himself. There we find what he is like, what hinders us from having a relationship with him, how he has addressed that hindrance, and how we can continue in a relationship with him once we've entered it. To the degree that our children do not know the fullness of God's Word, to that degree they will not know God as fully as he wills to be known.

"The goal of my teaching is for my children to consistently apply the Word of God to their lives." True, God gave his Word so we would apply it, but there can be no shortcut to application that ignores the arduous task of learning what that Word contains. Before we can apply truth, we must know, comprehend, and accept it. We can only apply a biblical truth correctly when we understand it as God meant it. While we can begin to apply a tiny piece of truth as quickly as we learn it, our application will be much more accurate when we rightly understand its context—and, ultimately, the context of any biblical truth is the entire Bible. We will not wait until we know everything in the Bible before we begin to apply anything at all; still, the Bible is a book. It's not a box of fortune cookies. As with any book, we only know the whole when we rightly understand the parts. While our goal is application, there is a place for teaching our children Bible facts, stories, and content which they may not necessarily run out and apply this very afternoon. We can wait on application. We can teach content while our children are young, applying what we can now, but waiting for greater application later. If our children grow up with only a cursory idea of the high points of what the Bible contains, how can we expect them to accurately apply God's Word to their lives?

"What I hope to pass on to my children is a heart for the kingdom of God. I want them to have a passion for Christian mission and service." When Jesus came announcing that the kingdom of God was at hand, he relied on the entire Old Testament as the background for his words. He expected that people knew what he meant because he expected

they knew the Scriptures. Can your children care about the kingdom of God as Jesus meant it without a thorough understanding of what it is? From the Bible's perspective, what would it mean to "seek first" the kingdom of God? How will we—and our children—know this without a profound acquaintance with the Word of God, which is the source of this expression? And how will our children know they are serving God as he wants them to serve? Where will they find the motive and the power to persevere in a life of Christian mission and service when results are few and far between? We address these questions when we give our children roots that go down deep into Christian doctrine and biblical knowledge.

"I want my children to embrace the gospel for themselves and to share it with others." It took God the entire Old Testament to explain why we need the gospel and what to expect from it. It took him the whole New Testament to explain what it is, what it cost him, what it does for those who believe it, how we appropriate it, and how we don't. Can our children understand, appreciate, and love the gospel as they should, let alone have the words to articulate it to others, if they have not come to know and understand what God has taken care to communicate about it in his Word?

"It's very simple; I want my children to love Jesus. I want them to live for him, to seek and serve him." Which Jesus? Almost everyone agrees that Jesus was a real human being who lived and died in history. But was he a good teacher and a virtuous man, or was he God in the flesh? Was he the unfortunate victim of violence or the deliberate Savior of the world? Is he really the only way to God and why? Who is he and what has he done that makes him able to save? People have argued for centuries about who Jesus is and what he did. What if our children end up loving an idea of Jesus that isn't really Jesus at all, as so many people do, and they never know the difference? How can they avoid this if they are not thoroughly acquainted with the Word in written form, which alone reveals the Word made flesh?

The attaining of any of the goals in our list requires a firm, solid foundation of knowledge and doctrine. Our children cannot apply Scripture without knowing what it says. They cannot love Christ without knowing who he is. They can't obey God without knowing what he has commanded. And they will not know these things if we do not provide deliberate, thorough, rigorous instruction, just as we would do for subjects like math or grammar.

We need to cling to every one of the worthwhile goals in our list. But we also need to back up a step and acknowledge the priority of—yes, I'm going to say it—*filling children's heads with knowledge* of Christian truth. God could have ordained for us the ability to simply intuit truth about him—but he didn't (although most Americans act as though he did). He ordained a book, studied like any book, as the primary means of acquiring knowledge of God. Yes, we may rely on the Holy Spirit to bring to our children's minds what they need to know when they need to know it, but God has ordained Word and Spirit to operate together. In his usual way of working, the Spirit will not bring to our children's minds what has never been put into them.

We worry that if our children don't act on each piece of biblical information we give them, they are not making proper use of God's truth. We need to realize that, with children, a large part of our teaching must have, as its goal, the simple provision of information to believe. If our children possess an adequate, Christ-centered, biblical belief system, we can guide them in applying it now, and they can find ways to apply it again and again later, all through life. In one sense, right believing is its own application. Immediate "practical applications" can never substitute for a comprehensive grid of Christian thought against which to measure every life event. A piano teacher requires his students to master scales. This is a prerequisite for all the complex works the student will go on to play later. The scales, well-learned, provide the automatic reflex on which a life of music can be built. Christian doctrine, well-learned, gives children the skills they will need to examine each new idea, every sudden temptation, and each difficult decision as it comes along. Like drilling and practicing piano skills, learning such a system of truth will require time and concentrated effort. But it is worth doing! It does not need to be justified by a demonstration of how it can be applied right this minute.[4]

Why Know

- The knowledge of God is the most profound knowledge the human race has; it requires diligent study.
- God has revealed himself in a book. Knowing him well begins with knowing that book well.
- Applying biblical truth begins with knowing that truth.
- Seeking God's kingdom requires a scriptural understanding of what that kingdom is.
- Realizing how to serve God faithfully and staying motivated to do so depend on knowing God's will and promises.
- True understanding of, appreciation for, and belief in the gospel come from knowing what God has revealed about it in his Word.
- We know Jesus, the Word of God incarnate, through Scripture, the Word of God written.
- Every spiritual goal we have for our children requires a foundation of Christian knowledge.
- God has ordained Word and Spirit to work together.
- A thorough belief system based on knowledge of Scripture can be applied over and over, throughout life.

DO WE REALLY NEED TO MAKE SUCH STUDENTS OF OUR KIDS?

In an excellent article in *Modern Reformation*, Rev. Dr. Brian Lee addresses the argument that a more rigorous, more academic Christianity is only for those who like that sort of thing—seminary students and theology geeks and, in the words of his article's title, "eggheads."[5] If intellectual study is what those types like, says the argument, let them have

4. The scales illustration comes from John H. Walton and Kim E. Walton, *The Bible Story Handbook: A Resource for Teaching 175 Stories from the Bible* (Wheaton, IL: Crossway, 2010), 18.
5. Brian Lee, "Is Reformation Christianity Just for Eggheads?," *Modern Reformation* 21, no. 5 (September/October 2012): 16–20.

it, but they have no right to require the rest of us ordinary Christians to memorize catechisms or study doctrine—or study anything for that matter. Dr. Lee refers to the often heard half-truth that biblical Christianity is a matter of the heart, not the head. After all, says this argument, don't we find in Acts 4:13 that learned religious leaders marveled at Peter and John's bold defense, knowing they were "uneducated, common men" who had simply "been with Jesus"? The mistake that both the religious leaders and this argument make comes in assuming that *being with Jesus* refers to some kind of warm, so-happy-together emotion. We must remember that Jesus chose his apostles to be with him for the purpose of *learning* from him (see Mark 3:14; 4:33–34). Jesus' primary priority was teaching. Being with Jesus meant exposure, 24/7, to one who spoke of God and heaven from experience (John 3:11–13). Somehow, we've missed the point that the religious leaders, in thinking the apostles were uneducated, were *incorrect*. They knew the apostles were fishermen, tax collectors, commoners, and the like. They knew they had not received formal, religious training in the rabbinical schools. But these "common" men had spent three years, night and day, with Jesus Christ himself. Once Jesus had risen, he waited to return to heaven, "appearing to them during forty days and speaking about the kingdom of God" (Acts 1:3). "And beginning with Moses and all the prophets, he interpreted to them in all the Scriptures the things concerning himself" (Luke 24:27). He told them, " 'Everything written about me in the Law of Moses and the Prophets and the Psalms must be fulfilled.' Then he opened their minds to understand the Scriptures" (vv. 44–45). Apostles ("sent ones") were first of all disciples, and the word *disciple* means *learner*. As he prepared to leave them, Jesus told his followers not just to baptize, not just to make converts, but to make disciples, to teach people of all nations to observe all he had commanded. People marveled at the arguments and the teaching of the apostles because no one knew where they had received such intense training in the Scriptures, but receive it they had.

Dr. Lee reminds us in his article that revelation through a book that would require study was God's idea. When God first wrote the Ten Commandments on tablets of stone, how many people in that great crowd of Hebrew ex-slaves could read? Yet God chose to reveal himself through words Moses wrote at his command. On through the following centuries, God commanded his prophets and inspired his apostles to write. Consequently, when God requires his people to know, love, and obey his Word and to teach it to their children, he's requiring them to read, to reread, to study, and to memorize.

This, I contend, is what we're missing as we seek to train and disciple children. We take them to church, we pray with them at meals or at bedtime, we seek to mold their characters and build certain habits, we listen to and read experts who provide tips on training and discipline. But we don't methodically teach our children Bible content and Christian doctrine. We fail to familiarize them with the book God has given and with the truths he has revealed.

Why Know

- Jesus chose disciples and taught them well, then commissioned them to go on to teach others.
- God chose to reveal himself through a book, which he requires us to know through hearing it preached, reading it, studying it, and memorizing it.

THE CURRENT SAD STATE OF AFFAIRS

Christian Smith, professor of sociology at the University of Notre Dame, was the principal investigator for the National Study of Youth and Religion, a research project conducted from 2001 to 2005, with the religious experiences of American youth as its subject. Smith's findings, in a technical and controlled way, demonstrate what I have seen on an informal, daily basis in my years of teaching junior high and high school students. Most of the teens I teach freely call themselves Christians. Some have given testimonies at their baptisms. They accept what their parents have taught them and what they have been taught by the churches that they attend regularly. In the American teens Smith interviewed for his study, he found the same overall positive attitude toward the religion of their families that I usually see in my students. In his book, however, he laments what I also observe regularly: he labels most teens "incredibly inarticulate" about their religious beliefs. It isn't simply that they find it difficult to explain what they believe. As you question students further, Smith says, it is the beliefs themselves that are vague at best and often actually in disagreement with the faith traditions teens claim to hold.[6]

Smith cites many examples. A conservative Protestant boy's summary of his religion was, "I'm sure God exists and, like, helps people and answers their prayers, that's pretty much it." A conservative Protestant girl asserted that God had done a lot of good in her life. When pressed for examples, she said, "I don't know," then, "I, well, I have a house, parents, I have the Internet, I have a phone, I have cable." Concerning basic Protestant ideas regarding how to be right with God, evangelical teens held quite *un*evangelical ideas. A fifteen-year-old conservative Protestant boy put it this way: "If you do the right thing and don't do anything bad, I mean nothing really bad, you know you'll go to heaven. If you don't then you're screwed [laughs], that's about it." A sixteen-year-old Protestant girl gave this explanation: "Being a Christian means, um, don't do many sins, read the Bible, go to church, living godly, that's about it. It's basically not committing sin, basically."[7]

I find the same thing in my much smaller group of teens that Smith claims for American teens at large: they claim to believe, and they claim their beliefs to be vitally important to them, but they have little familiarity with the truths they claim to believe. This raises the question: can our children really believe what they do not even know? Theologian and seminary professor David F. Wells writes that in many contemporary Christian churches, "Religious words have . . . , more or less, disappeared . . . words like: 'justification,' 'atonement,' 'judgment,' 'holiness,' 'incarnation,' 'sanctification,' and 'glorification.' If the words have gone, so too have the doctrines of which the words were a part and by which the doctrines were taught."[8] Centuries ago, John Calvin wrote, "Of what avail was it to

6. Christian Smith, *Soul Searching: The Religious and Spiritual Lives of American Teenagers* (New York: Oxford University Press, 2005), 131–34.

7. Ibid., 135–36.

8. David Wells, *The Courage to Be Protestant: Truth-Lovers, Marketers, and Emergents in the Postmodern World* (Grand Rapids: Wm. B. Eerdmans Publishing Co., 2008), 53.

profess respect for the gospel and not to know what it meant? . . . With Christians, where there is no knowledge, there is no faith."[9]

As Christian Smith sees it, the "Christian" youth he interviewed had a positive enough impression of Christianity, but they lacked an effective education in its truths. He writes, "The majority of U.S. teens would badly fail a hypothetical short-answer or essay test on the beliefs of their religion."[10]

Smith found that few American youth see religion as having truths they must believe and demands they must obey. Rather, young people understand religion—and therefore, God—as something that exists to help them when they have special needs, remaining politely out of the way in ordinary life. With teen after teen, of many denominational backgrounds, Smith found the same idea of religion. His findings were so consistent that Smith gave a name to this religion held by so many. He named it Moralistic Therapeutic Deism (MTD).[11] American teens' religion is *moralistic* because one of its central tenets is this: a person's well-being depends on being nice, respecting others, demonstrating responsibility, and working hard at improving oneself. This religion is *therapeutic* because of teens' misguided belief that Christianity is all about them. It exists to give them what they need to make them feel good. It's there to help them when they're frightened or when they feel inadequate. Its purpose is to supply whatever is lacking to make them happy and peaceful. Finally, Smith calls teens' religion *deism* because, while teens believe in a moral creator God, they don't see him as involved in daily life or as making demands; their God only acts when people call on him to help because a serious problem has arisen. Smith claims, "The language, and therefore experience, of Trinity, holiness, sin, grace, justification, sanctification, church, Eucharist, and heaven and hell appear, among most Christian teenagers in the United States at the very least, to be supplanted by the language of happiness, niceness, and an earned heavenly reward."[12]

9. John Calvin commenting on Gal. 1:8 in his *Commentary on Galatians and Ephesians* (Grand Rapids: Christian Classics Ethereal Library), http://www.ccel.org/ccel/calvin/calcom41.i.html.

10. Smith, *Soul Searching*, 137.

11. Ibid., 162–65.

12. Ibid., 171.

Why Know

- America's "Christian" kids claim to believe Christianity, but many of them cannot articulate what it teaches.
- Our kids can't really believe truth they do not know.

HOW HAS THIS HAPPENED AND WHAT CAN WE DO ABOUT IT?

How could this have happened? Smith suggests that one of the most important paths down which American youth culture has traveled is that of therapeutic individualism, in which the self is all-important and external authority is of little consequence. Teens have been trained to esteem self, to realize self, to improve self, to trust self, and to help self. Christianity calls for exalting Christ, humbling and denying self, trusting God, and relying on the Holy Spirit. American children, even "Christian" American children, fail to think of God as one to whose demands they must submit. Rather, as they understand it, God's whole *raison d'être* is to grant them happiness and fulfillment. This message comes from all directions and must be countered with large doses of biblical truth.

David Wells has written extensively, tracing the history of how the Western church has chipped away at the truth that should serve as its very foundation. He challenges contemporary American Protestantism to return to the doctrinal seriousness it has given away in its attempt to appeal to the people of our postmodern world. Certainly we see that loss of doctrinal seriousness in what so many American churches offer to attract children and youth. Fun and entertainment take priority so kids will come, leaving only enough time for a tacked-on Bible story or a quick "Here's-how-God-can-make-you-feel-better" devotion at the end. "When our knowledge of God's truth is diminished, our understanding of God is diminished," Wells cautions.[13] "Christianity is not just an experience, we need to remember, but it is about truth."[14] Wells lists the Christian doctrines of creation, God, the nature of man, sin

13. Wells, *The Courage to Be Protestant*, 18.
14. Ibid., 45.

31

and the fall, redemption, Christ and his incarnation, the atonement, reconciliation, and grace, given by God in the Bible. He points out that, without knowing these things, there is no real understanding of God and his salvation. Wells laments that Western Christianity does not consider Bible knowledge a priority. This would explain the comment of one of my students, a delightful teen boy from a family committed to involvement in an evangelical church with a strong emphasis on missions. When asked in history class who Abraham was and what he had to do with ancient Israel, he said, with no trace of embarrassment, "I don't know much about the Bible; I never read it."

And yet the Bible is the book God gave us. He wants both us and our children to know it. It is truth. We want our children to believe, to apply, and to love that truth, but they must, first of all, know it. If, as I find, even American teens from evangelical and Reformed backgrounds are as incoherent and confused in the realm of spiritual truth as Christian Smith says they are, what can we do to arrest this disturbing phenomenon? Christian Smith's answer is to exhort parents and churches to stop being bashful about *teaching* their young people. He notes that teens can be quite clear on expressing truth related to drugs, drinking, STDs, and safe sex, subjects "about which they had been *drilled*" (his word, my emphasis). When it comes to faith and religion, Smith observes, adults hang back from teaching. Parents provide a little, but not too much, exposure to their beliefs, while churches often substitute entertainment in place of education for their young. But children and teens *need* Christian education, to remove the ignorance and misunderstanding they have when left to themselves, and to lay a foundation of truth and doctrine on which to build for the future.[15]

Why Know

- At its very heart, Christianity is a set of propositional truths to be known and believed.
- Without diligent instruction, children and teens will have only ignorance and misunderstanding in the things of God.

15. Smith, *Soul Searching*, 267.

JUST DO IT!

When parents and teachers become convinced that, yes, their children need to learn Bible—the Bible's big picture, its individual narratives, its characters, its genres, its commands and promises, its doctrines, its gospel in all its fullness—or when they become convinced that they must instruct their children in the rich doctrinal truths of the Christian faith, two worries may surface. One worry is that this kind of teaching will take big chunks of time. I agree. It will. There is no way around this. It takes time to chauffeur our children to soccer practice, wait with them through the practice, and drive them to all the matches. It takes time to take our children to their piano lessons every week, and, if the children don't spend time practicing daily, we've wasted the money we spent on the lessons. It takes time to make sure our children acquire competency in math, as we supply regular instruction for them, drill them on math facts, and make them finish assignments before they go play. Can we learn anything without spending time at it? The answer to this concern is not easy in our modern, overstimulated culture, but it is simple. *Make the time* to give your children (or students) rigorous, diligent instruction in the Bible and in Christian doctrine. You don't have to teach it all overnight; you can take years to teach, then go back through and reteach. But find or create a plan, and then work your plan. Purposefully teach the whole Bible, in its broad overview and in its details, to your children. Choose a method for making sure they are learning the doctrines of the Christian faith well enough that they will be able to articulate them back to someone. Then find thirty to sixty minutes several times a week to work through these plans with your children. Forget about one-minute Bibles or five-minute Bibles or any other promises to teach the Bible in leftover minutes we won't even notice, and *make the time* to teach your children Bible and doctrine.

The other worry that can surface when parents and teachers realize they need to exercise greater diligence in teaching their children is the concern that they themselves don't know the Bible and Christian doctrine all that well; how, then, can they teach it to their children? Some how-tos and a list of resources, both for your own learning and for teaching your children, will come later in this book. For now, though, I'll say this. The answer to this worry is similar to the one for the concern about time constraints. Just begin. Begin somewhere. Begin to educate yourself and, at the same time, begin teaching your children. Find one of the many Bible reading plans available and/or a good commentary or two, or a comprehensive study Bible you can trust, and begin to get to know God's Word. Get acquainted with some of the classic creeds, confessions, and catechisms of the Protestant church, or read some of the many authors who can help you to not only understand, but also to love, theology and doctrine. One bonus of making a commitment to teaching your children is this: the best way to learn anything well is to teach it to others. Even just memorizing a catechism along with your children will open to you whole new worlds in understanding the riches of the Christian faith.

Head knowledge—Bible characters, events, places, and stories; propositional truths; specific doctrines spelled out in confessions and catechisms—this is what I'm begging Christian parents and teachers to learn to value once again as they teach their children. Biblical, doctrinal, Christian knowledge is the foundation of all we long for our children to have. If their religion consists of experience or emotions or good behavior, their religion will crumble in the end.

In the introduction to their book *Give Them Grace: Dazzling Your Kids with the Love of Jesus*, Elyse Fitzpatrick and Jessica Thompson write, "It's the premise of this book that the primary reason that the majority of kids from Christian homes stray from the faith is that they never really heard it or had it to begin with. They were taught that God wants them to be good, that poor Jesus is sad when they disobey, and that asking Jesus into their heart is the breadth and depth of the gospel message. Scratch the surface of the faith of the young people around you and you'll find a disturbing deficiency of understanding of even the most basic tenets of Christianity."[16] The authors go on to explain how parents can demonstrate the gospel all day, every day, in how they teach, discipline,

---

16. Elyse Fitzpatrick and Jessica Thompson, *Give Them Grace: Dazzling Your Kids with the Love of Jesus* (Wheaton, IL: Crossway, 2011), 18.

and correct their children. These authors would never be content with Bible facts and doctrinal content alone for children, and neither am I. I only plead that parents and teachers take care to instill those facts and that content as an adequate foundation on which to build all the rest.

Don't be afraid of head knowledge. Supply it for your children in great quantity, beginning when they are young and able to absorb so much so easily. By all means, seek loving hearts for your children. Train them in godly character. Nurture them in spiritual maturity. Show them how to apply the Bible's teaching to life. But don't neglect to jump with them, head first, into the biblical and doctrinal *knowledge* they need.

Why Know

- Christianity based on experience or emotion or good behavior will crumble in the face of life's trials.
- Teaching Bible and doctrine to children will require a significant time commitment, but it will be time well spent, for both teacher and student.

2

Truth: The Lifeboat
for Future Storms

There is a reason that the Eeyore collection in my classroom grew every Christmas, augmented by gifts. Students and relatives alike recognized that Eeyore was something of a kindred spirit to me. We can both discern the dark and the dour in the sunniest moments. My Eeyore-like tendencies have diminished over the years, tempered by growth in the knowledge of God's goodness and grace, but I still believe in taking a look at life every now and then from Eeyore's perspective. Such imagining causes us to consider if the truths on which we have built our lives would sustain us if our lives were altogether different.

Calvin Coolidge famously said, "If you see ten troubles coming down the road, you can be sure that nine will run into the ditch before they reach you."[1] He's right; there is no point in worrying about the future. Still, we must recognize that temptation and trial are commonplaces of life in our fallen world. The question is not whether our children *will* have to suffer; the questions are only when, and how severely? When they do, what will they have to carry them through? To what will they cling in order to make their way in the dark?

I contend that a robust theology, a strong, well-connected belief system, is the most helpful thing we can give our children to prepare them for the suffering they will inevitably face as they live in a world spoiled by sin. When, like the disciples in the boat, our children experience

1. Listed in a series of sayings by "Silent Cal" in Michael R. Lowman, *United States History: A Heritage of Freedom* (Pensacola, FL: A Beka Book, 2009), 413.

storms that make them wonder if Jesus cares that they're perishing, a strong belief system can serve as the safety net to catch them as they stumble. A biblical worldview, so familiar that it acts as their default way of thinking, can still uphold them when all their other systems crash. Yes, they will need more than *just* the correct beliefs. They will need, at some point, to choose to hold to these truths and to act upon them. But the beliefs must be there in the first place. When our adult children are hit so hard by temptation or trial that, for the moment, they cannot think through the choices at all, those beliefs must be such a part of them as to be an almost automatic guidance system for them.

We hope our children will grow up to be adults who love Christ more than anything, and, for the purpose of this chapter, let's assume that will be the case. Even as Christians, sometimes precisely *because* they're Christians, our children will face difficult days. Christianity has enough depth to stand up to the most searching tests they will encounter. Are they learning those depths now? A vague belief in a God who is good and who desires good things for us, who wants us to be kind to each other and is grieved when we're not, will not prove adequate when circumstances lead them to the brink of despair. Are we equipping our children with a faith substantial enough to pull them through their toughest trials?

When we look to the future of our children, we imagine good things. Whether they are infants or teens, we see their future through a rosy glow, typical, I believe, of modern Western Christianity. For decades, now, Americans have viewed Christianity as a religion that makes this present life better for its adherents. Well-meaning evangelists often present the gospel in terms of a solution to a here-and-now problem. Are you lonely? Jesus will be your friend. Do you feel like a failure? Jesus will accept you and give you success you never imagined. Are you discouraged, defeated, depressed? Jesus will open to you a life of deepest joy. And, at the same time, pastors and teachers have tackled every imaginable problem and offered teaching on how to overcome it via Christian principles. Can't meet your budget? Having marital tensions? Don't like your boss? Dealing with angry teenagers? Feeling unhappy? Low self-esteem? Each of those things and every other real-life problem you can think of have been made into a sermon series or a Sunday school class. It has become normal to think of the Christian life as inherently happy, victorious, and successful. Jesus solves problems. Following him, we can find the answers and know the formulas that will give us and our families health, happiness, and, if not extreme wealth, at least adequate prosperity.

In this chapter, I would like to challenge you to briefly put on an imaginary pair of Eeyore-glasses and look with me at some of the heartaches that could touch our children as they make their way through a fallen world. Compare what they're learning now, at home and at church, with what they will need then, and see if we're equipping them as we should be.

Why Know

- Strong, well-known Christian truth can provide a safety net for our adult children when they are severely tried or tempted.

THE FUTURE THROUGH EEYORE'S EYES

We all hope that our children will succeed in their chosen careers and live financially independent lives, fulfilled in their work. For many such careers in America, college education has become a prerequisite. However, for all kinds of reasons, your child may not complete the college education of his choice. College classes may prove to be beyond either his academic ability or his economic ability. Or she might complete her chosen degree, after racking up substantial debt, but find no job in her field. Given all the unknowns, it is possible that your adult child will end up in a very basic job, one that pays the bills, but offers little personal satisfaction. Will he have a belief system strong enough to carry him with joy and hope through day after day of drudgery? Or perhaps the only job available doesn't pay enough. Perhaps there is no job of any kind to be found. For all kinds of reasons, the maybe-not-extravagant-but-at-least-comfortable home we envision for our adult children, where happy children of their own practice piano in the living room or play soccer in the backyard, may never become a reality. Our children may struggle with intense financial difficulties. I know that Christian courses in wise financial management abound, and that applying biblical principles can make a tremendous difference, but human beings cannot control every circumstance. Economic disasters occur, on both a national and an individual scale. Surely some of the farmers who left their farms in the Dust Bowl were responsible Christians who could no longer hang on in the face of the disaster that hit them. Surely some of the people who, through sudden illness or injury, face enormous medical bills and no way to earn an income, have been diligent, prudent Christians. It is at least a possibility that your children, as adults, will endure economic hardship, even poverty. What God has revealed about himself in his Word can fortify them to face such circumstances, provided they know what he has revealed.

We assume our children will meet and fall in love with Christian spouses; we have prayed for that since before they were born. We envision the weddings, with all our friends and family around us, rejoicing in these new, godly unions that will be sources of joy for many. We hope our married children will live near enough to us for regular visits, but, even if we can only gather for the occasional holiday dinner or family reunion, we imagine good times of Christian fellowship around our future table.

Most people marry. Yet, throughout history, there have been—and still, today, there are—godly, committed Christians who have never found a Christian spouse. What if your child should be one of those? It's not the end of the world; in fact, my single friends would tell me there are some distinct advantages to singleness (the apostle Paul made the same point, once), but it does bring its own unique challenges. What if year succeeds year, and your son's circle of friends continues to diminish because all his companions of younger days find female companions and establish new lifestyles? Might he have a sense that life is passing him by? As your daughter stands as a bridesmaid by one after another of her friends and never gets to stand in the place of bride herself, might she begin to wonder what's wrong with her that no one has ever asked for *her* hand in marriage? How will your son handle the dawning realization, as he celebrates his thirtieth and fortieth birthdays, that he will probably never marry? How will your daughter deal with the solitude of a silent home to return to every night? Where will your single children find the encouragement in Christian living that they need when every small group seems to be for couples and there's no one at home to talk them through their discouragements and temptations? No doubt as you and your church train your children, you look to the future and you seek to build into them the character that will be needed to make them good spouses. But have you considered what you're giving them to equip them for lives of singleness, if that should be their lot, with its attendant disappointment, loneliness, and temptation to bitterness and to sexual sin? Christianity has adequate answers for living a single life with joy, but singles will need to have those answers deeply engrained within for the days when living with contentment is a struggle.

Your child may fall in love with a godly person and receive counsel from you and other Christians whom they know well, and then marry. Suppose, then, that your child finds, to his or her astonishment and to the astonishment of all who watch, that this person is not what he or she seemed to be. While this is not likely where people are careful, it does happen. Hidden details may come to light that would have given your child pause before marrying, but now it's too late; or, being a sinner in a fallen world, the spouse may change in ways that hurt the marriage. Perhaps a mean streak surfaces that had not been seen before, or at least a moodiness that kills communication. Perhaps the spouse develops irresponsible spending habits, making it difficult for your child to carry out financial responsibilities. Your daughter doesn't have what she needs to buy the children's clothing and school supplies because of the way her husband likes to entertain his friends, or your son cannot stay out of debt with a wife who shops and never drops. For a host of reasons, relations may deteriorate and, even though your child might be willing to seek Christian counsel, the spouse will not. Your child faces a different kind of loneliness from his single counterpart—the loneliness of a stressful marriage. Your child may discover, early in the marriage or late, that he or she is bound for life to someone with whom there is no longer any sense of companionship, let alone romance. Or the person you and your child saw as the answer to years of prayer for a Christian spouse might decide, over time, that he or she is not a Christian after all and wants to get out of the marriage. A husband decides he doesn't like the responsibility that accompanies marriage and family and leaves. A wife finds that another man makes her feel more romantic and chooses to live with him instead.

Marriage is a gift, and we prepare our children to work at it and to enjoy it. All of God's Word, the encouragement and support of God's people, and the Holy Spirit himself provide our married children with resources far beyond merely their own to enable their marriages to glorify Christ. And still, we cannot guarantee happy marriages for our children. In the culture we live in, we have to recognize the possibility that our adult children may one day be the suffering partners in difficult or even failed marriages. If, in God's good providence, this should be the lot of our children, what will keep them from falling into bitterness and despair and enable them to continue to glorify and enjoy God in the midst of such pain? A solid grasp of the character, the purposes, and the promises of God, as seen in the details of his Word, will go a long way to sustaining injured spouses in an unhealthy marriage.

How many of us count debilitating disease as one of the things for which we should prepare our children? It's one thing when children have had health issues all along, as their parents prepare them to live with those issues in adulthood. But sometimes illness sets in later in life, after years of good health and after rigorous study and satisfying work in a chosen field. The illness may linger, worsening through time, and forcing your son into premature retirement. How will he cope, not only with the loss of income, but with the abrupt halt to work he had enjoyed? The illness could prove so severe that most ordinary activities become impossible. What if the world moves on, while both a walk around the block and a trip to the store require better health than your daughter possesses? When bodies are too weak to join God's people in worship or even to read Scripture on one's own, from what source will your child pull the strength to sustain his or her spirit? If pain becomes a constant so that sleep can only be snatched for an hour or two at a time, where will your son find rest? When surgery follows surgery and nothing is ever resolved, where will your daughter find courage? When, at first, friends pray fervently for healing which never comes, and then lose interest and drift away, how will our children not end up embittered and angry?

In times of prolonged pain, our children's emotions will tell them that they cannot go on. They will need something outside of themselves to cling to if they are going to stay afloat in difficulty this deep. Solid doctrine, certain and sure; objective truth, revealed by God for just such a time as this—these can buoy up those whose feelings, experiences, and intuition cannot bear the weight of pain that doesn't go away. Christian truth insists that God rules the universe and ordains all that happens. It assures us that, not only does he always know exactly what is best, but he loves his own too much to let anything but the best touch them. Christian truth maintains that, when we begin to doubt God's love, we can look to the cross of Christ and see that love spelled out in inarguable terms. This truth is what our children need. They need it in all its fullness, with all the details that support it and make it solid and substantial enough to use against feelings no longer under control.

Debilitating illness may strike your child's spouse, not your child, altering the marriage beyond recognition. Your daughter, who had dreamed of managing a home and teaching her children, might have to become the breadwinner for the family. Will she have what she needs to blossom under such demands? Perhaps, just when your son has launched a promising career in a field for which he is ideally suited, his wife develops a serious physical condition. He might have to let his career slip from his fingers while he devotes more attention to the needs of his family. What foundation will he stand on as he rejoices in the lot he has received? How will he hold back his disappointment and model the love of Christ for his bride in the ongoing, daily strain? A firm grasp of the big-picture plan of redemptive history—what God has been doing and will do for his glory—will help your children accept and rejoice in the place appointed for them, even when it isn't what they would have chosen.

Illness may hit one or more of your grandchildren. If so, our adult children will ache to watch the suffering of this vulnerable little person who looks to them for relief. As the years go by and there are few offers of childcare for sick or disabled children, what will give parents the refreshment they need to return, again and again, to caring for this needy person who depends on them? Can they continue, sturdy in hope, when no chance of a normal adulthood presents itself for their child? Will they have the answers they need to extinguish fear of the future?

All parents would like to believe that, if they merely do all God has called them to do (merely!), their children will grow up serving the Lord. But no parent will do all that God has called him or her to do, and, when God saves, it's never because we've been excellent parents. Sometimes parents diligently teach and faithfully train, but the children themselves, individuals who make choices, grow up to reject Christ or even to commit crimes. We recoil from the very idea, yet our adult children could face this with their own children, our grandchildren. What then? Will it destroy our children's confidence in Christianity? Will it turn them from God? A lifeline we can throw from here to our children in the future, a lifeline that will be there waiting for them when they need it, is a sure and certain knowledge of God's wisdom, power, and goodness, along with the big picture of the promised redemption of his people. Here our children will be able to stand and to keep their heads above the storm waves that threaten to destroy them.

We don't know what the future holds for our children. They may be in the very place that a tornado, a flood, or an earthquake hits. They may endure moments or hours of terror as a result. They may lose loved ones in horrific circumstances. They may return home to find no home left standing. Their dazed senses will struggle for an answer to why an omnipotent God did not stop this when he could have; would your children have something to hold to then? Millions of Christians in the world at this very moment live in the midst of war, or endure, occasionally or even often, attacks by terrorists. While we may have little fear of that in our country at this moment, do we have guarantees that our children will not serve in the military and see war, or that they will not find themselves, several decades from now, in situations completely other than the prosperous peace in which they grew up? If, one day, our children come face to face with the brutality humans can inflict on other humans, will their convictions and their certainties enable them to support such a burden? Will they be able to continue confident that this will not last, that God's glorious kingdom will triumph in the end? Will they have the essentials for waiting out the evil and for refusing admittance into their own souls of the dark shadow it casts while they wait?

If no other heartache touches our children, they will all, surely, encounter that great enemy of mankind, death. One day, our children will lose someone they love. They may have to endure long, lonely nights and days of watching someone die, a pre-death grief that remembers what this person was and mourns for what he or she has become. When death finally comes, they will have to learn to live with the hole in their lives that has taken the place of someone they loved. And, unless they remain until Christ returns, our children will one day face their own dying and death. Will they automatically fall back on words such as "What is your only comfort in life and in death? That I am not my own, but belong—body and soul, in life and in death—to my faithful Savior, Jesus Christ,"[2] or on Jesus' words, "Fear not, I am the first and the last, and the living one. I died, and behold, I am alive forevermore, and I have the keys of Death and Hades" (Rev. 1:17–18)?

Why Know

- A strong belief system can provide joy and hope through days of drudgery.
- A deep knowledge of who God is makes it easier to trust him through economic hardship.
- Awareness of Christian truth can bring contentment to a life of singleness.

2. Q&A 1 in Faith Alive Christian Resources, *The Heidelberg Catechism: 450th Anniversary Edition* (Faith Alive Christian Resources, 2013), 8.

- Christian spouses in unhappy or failed marriages can continue in hope when they have a solid grasp of the character, promises, and purposes of God.
- The assurance that God rules the universe, ordains all that happens, and acts in love toward his children strengthens those who must endure debilitating illness.
- Our adult children will be able to rejoice in the place appointed for them, even when it isn't what they would have chosen, if they have a firm grasp of redemptive history and God's purposes in it.
- A sure knowledge of God's wisdom, power, and goodness helps Christian parents trust God with their children's lives.
- With a clear awareness of God's promises for a future judgment and a new heaven and earth, God's people can wait out the suffering that comes from natural disaster or from human cruelty.
- Knowledge of the risen Christ fortifies God's people when they face their own deaths or the deaths of those they love.

PARTICULARLY CHRISTIAN TRIALS

Perhaps you're already reeling after such a list of potential miseries! And yet, so far, we have only considered the basic, garden-variety type of trial that people in any place in any era might encounter. There are specific trials that *Christian* people, throughout the centuries, have had to endure. In many countries today, Christians suffer intense persecution that we, here in the United States, have never known. A 2012 Pew Forum report indicated that three-fourths of the world's seven billion people live where religious liberty faces significant social or political restriction. Much of the persecution and violence that exists targets Christians.[3] If our children were to meet the particular kind of suffering that is religious persecution, would they be equipped with the truth that would sustain them? Again, just *knowing* truth is no guarantee that people will choose to suffer for Christ if the choice is put to them. But knowing the truth will make clear the reason why the suffering is worth it. Knowing the truth and returning to it over and over will provide a

3. Thomas Kidd, "Numbered Victims," *WORLD*, June 29, 2013, 86.

great measure of comfort in that word's older sense of fortifying and making strong to endure.

Throughout the world, Christianity's enemies are legion—and they exercise great power. In Communist countries, atheistic governments demand of their citizens a devotion owed only to the divine. When Christians insist on worshiping and obeying their Lord, their own governments persecute, imprison, and enslave them. Christian minorities in Muslim countries all over the world live in daily fear of bombings, beatings, church fires, and machete attacks, often with no legal consequences to the assailants. Guerrillas and drug lords in South America, lawmakers and academics in secular Western nations, traditional animists in isolated tribes—all unite around this one commitment: Christianity must be silenced.

For a long time, American evangelicals have been able to live with no experiential knowledge of these things. Those who read history, however, must realize that governments rise and fall. Trends in the thinking of entire nations come and go. The comfortable, Christianity-friendly lifestyle Americans have enjoyed for so long will not last forever. There are fresh accounts daily of escalating hostility to Christian thought and expression all over the world. Faithfulness to the teaching of Scripture grows increasingly unacceptable and, in some cases, illegal, even in Western democracies.

D. A. Carson has written an important book for the twenty-first century entitled *The Intolerance of Tolerance*. In it, he demonstrates how the definition of *tolerance* has changed. In the past, dictionaries defined the verb *tolerate* as "to permit; to not interfere with; to recognize and respect (others' beliefs, practices, etc.)." While rejecting someone's beliefs or practices, the tolerant individual still respected the person and acknowledged his right to hold and to argue for his own opinion. Carson goes on to quote a more recent Encarta definition of the noun form of the word *tolerance*. It is the "*accepting* of the differing views of other people, e.g., in religious or political matters" (italics added). No longer is it a matter of allowing someone to hold an opinion differing from ours; tolerance now requires that we accept the contrary opinion itself. The only position that simply cannot be tolerated is the one that dares to suggest that a belief or a practice is wrong.[4] This has obvious implications for Christianity, as it rests firmly on the Bible as the very Word of God, correct and true on every matter it addresses. From its earliest beginnings in the Roman Empire, biblical Christianity has always insisted that Jesus Christ alone is Lord, and the only way to acceptance with God. As thinking moves more and more toward the new "tolerance" in matters of morality and religion, and as Christians continue to insist that what God has said on these matters is true and right, our society will become increasingly *intolerant* of Christian thought and practice.

The definition of *hate* has changed as well. *Hate speech* has come to include speech, no matter how courteous or respectful, that disagrees with certain positions or behavior. When television journalist Brit Hume was asked to comment on Tiger Woods's sex scandal, he quietly commented that Woods should consider the Christian religion, since the forgiveness he needed was not to be found in the Buddhism Woods embraced. Outrage exploded in the media.[5] In a number of Western countries, Christian speakers are forbidden by law to compare Christianity and Islam in a way that "vilifies" Islam, while no similar laws protecting Christianity have been passed.[6] Former Miss America, Carrie Prejean, was asked what she thought of gay marriage. She replied that "marriage should be between a man and a woman. No offense to anybody out there, but that's how I was raised." The response from Perez Hilton, a gay columnist, was to call Ms. Prejean "a dumb bitch with half a brain." Giuliana Ranic, news anchor for E!, called her "an ignorant disgrace" who "makes me sick to my stomach."[7] A twelve-year-old, who posted a video on YouTube against homosexuality because of the Bible's teaching, drew this response: "You, just like everyone who is against gay marriage, is a mentally retarded bigot. No exceptions. Now go to hell."[8]

4. D. A. Carson, *The Intolerance of Tolerance* (Grand Rapids: Wm. B. Eerdmans Publishing Co., 2012), 2–4.

5. Ibid., 43.

6. Ibid., 41.

7. Ibid., 40.

8. Michael L. Brown, *A Queer Thing Happened to America and What a Long, Strange Trip It's Been* (Concord, NC: EqualTime Books, 2011), 52.

This animosity toward the expression of Christian beliefs is having an increasing impact on Western thought and legislation. Photographers have been sued—and have lost in court—because they refused to participate in same-sex weddings by photographing them. Counselors, unwilling to affirm gay relationships, have been fired for offering to refer counselees in those relationships to other counselors. In July 2010, an adjunct professor of Catholicism at the University of Illinois was fired for saying that homosexual acts are wrong according to Catholic teaching.[9]

"In the name of tolerant diversity and a free press," Carson writes, "the agenda of hidden motives surfaces: a targeted contempt for and hatred of Christ and Christians, a contempt and hatred reserved for no other religion."[10]All indications lead us to believe that we are only going to see this targeted contempt and hatred grow. In a recent article in *WORLD* magazine, Edward Lee Pitts described what he called "the marginalization of Christianity in a [United States] military becoming more and more hostile to religion." He cited as examples the prohibition against Christian prayers in funeral services for veterans at Houston's National Cemetery, a chaplain rebuked by his superior for ending his prayer with the words "in Jesus' name," and an Army Reserve training brief on dangerous hate groups listing "evangelical Christians and Roman Catholics" along with al-Qaeda.[11] And, really, what should we expect? We in the West, and especially in the U.S., have enjoyed a long period of acceptance, respect, even admiration for Christian teaching. But what does Scripture predict? Jesus told his followers that, if the world hated him, it would certainly hate them (John 15:18–20). The apostle Paul assured Timothy that all who desire to live godly in Christ Jesus *will* be persecuted (2 Tim. 3:12).

Biblical Christians do not want to be hateful. They want—not just to be perceived to be, but truly—to *be* loving, kind, and forgiving. Our Lord calls us to this. We must be careful, though, not to let the world define "loving, kind, and forgiving" for us. The world would tell us

9. Ibid., 531–32.
10. Carson, *The Intolerance of Tolerance*, 93.
11. Edward Lee Pitts, "Holding the Line," *WORLD Magazine*, July 13, 2013, 34.

that, if we say certain behaviors are morally unacceptable when everyone else says they are not, we are harsh, judgmental, and hateful. The world would tell us that if we openly proclaim our faith as the only true faith, we are rude, unloving and—criticism of criticisms—*intolerant.*

In Christian Smith's interviews with teens, he discovered that American teens feel strongly that public discourse must be civil, and they detest "faith talk" that is rude and offensive. Teens, like all of us, have witnessed people claiming to hold the truths they cherish while speaking in obnoxious, insulting, and honestly hateful terms. Most of us want to distance ourselves from such people. But in their concern for showing respect for others, Smith writes in *Soul Searching*, teens have come to think that the only stance of civility is the one conceding that all religions are basically the same. They think that good manners prohibit anyone from claiming his faith tradition has something that others lack. What teens don't seem to realize, Smith points out, is that one can clearly articulate a well-thought-out faith with confidence *without* being rude and offensive. One can give reasons why another's position is wrong *and* demonstrate gracious courtesy to the person who holds it at the same time.[12] D. A. Carson agrees. He writes that Christians should be able to live and work and interact with people of all different persuasions, fighting for their freedom to believe according to their conscience and to express the opinions they hold. At the same time, as Christians called to proclaim the truth of God to all people, we must refuse to be silenced out of fear that if we say a religion is wrong or a behavior is immoral, we are using "hate speech." We allow for bad beliefs and for bad actions, and we speak out boldly about why they're bad; at the same time, we accept the people who hold or do them without hesitation, hoping and working toward their coming to faith and repentance.[13]

Mike Horton, writing of the imperative of loving our Muslim neighbors here in America, insists that while we must respect, befriend, and diligently defend Muslims' rights to believe as they wish, we must

12. Christian Smith, *Soul Searching: The Religious and Spiritual Lives of American Teenagers* (New York: Oxford University Press, 2009), 268.

13. Carson, *The Intolerance of Tolerance*, 6.

still acknowledge that their basic beliefs and ours contradict each other. They cannot both be true. Biblical Christians must be willing to love those who believe differently, *and* speak the truth about the differences. We must know those differences, though, and Horton writes that this will necessitate "a deeper commitment on the part of churches to help Christians know what they believe and why."[14]

If one day soon Christians, even in our country, will face some measure of persecution because of their beliefs, will our children be ready? Will they know the solid truth of the Bible and of orthodox Christian doctrine so well that the smooth reasoning and the angry accusations of the world will stand out to them as obviously, clearly *wrong*?

Christianity is a revealed religion, and its revelation comes to us in the Bible's historical narrative and doctrinal teaching. Yes, Christian truth must be applied and personally experienced. But Christianity is, first of all, God's revelation of truth. Christianity states that truth in propositions, creeds, and catechisms; there is substance to it. This substance is either true or false. And this truth, this substance, is found in a systematic study of Scripture. Our children will not be able to even hold to Christianity if they don't know it, let alone stand firm for it in the face of determined opposition. In the New Testament epistle bearing his name, Jude appealed to his readers "to contend for the faith that was once for all delivered to the saints" (Jude 3). This presupposes heads filled with the knowledge of the truths, the propositions, the doctrines, and the facts of that faith. Now, in the window of opportunity that we have, home and church together must teach our children the substance of Christianity. We do this when we provide for them a consistent, systematic study of doctrine and of Scripture. We want them to learn it well now, as children, so they will have it to hold to and to defend as adults.

Why Know

- A solid grasp of biblical truth gives persecuted believers the ability to see that Christianity is worth suffering for.

14. Michael Horton, "Christ and Islam," *Modern Reformation*, July/August 2012, 45.

- A thorough knowledge of God's Word enables Christians to understand what's wrong with the world's reasoning on issues where it disagrees with Scripture.
- Systematic study of Christianity's substance strengthens believers to hold to truth and to defend it when it's attacked.

THEOLOGY FOR A MARSHWIGGLE

In C. S. Lewis's *The Silver Chair*, one of the Narnia chronicles, Puddleglum, an odd-looking creature called a marshwiggle, is playing host to Eustace and Jill before they set out together on a quest commissioned by Aslan. Puddleglum is fishing, for eels, he explains, though he adds, "I shouldn't wonder if I didn't get any. And you won't like them much if I do." When Eustace asks why not, Puddleglum replies, "Why, it's not in reason that you should like our sort of victuals. . . . All the same, while I am a catching of them, if you two could try to light the fire—no harm trying—! The wood's behind the wigwam. It may be wet. You could light it inside the wigwam, and then we'd get all the smoke in our eyes. Or you could light it outside, and then the rain would come and put it out." Later, discussing the quest itself, Puddleglum dishes up more of the same. "It stands to reason we're not likely to get very far on a journey to the North, not at this time of the year, with the winter coming on soon and all. And an early winter too, by the look of things. But you mustn't let that make you downhearted. Very likely, what with enemies, and mountains, and rivers to cross, and losing our way, and next to nothing to eat, and sore feet, we'll hardly notice the weather. And if we don't get far enough to do any good, we may get far enough not to get back in a hurry." Eustace finally protests in a burst of temper at the absurdity of so many proposed difficulties.[15] You may well be protesting against me right now too, for holding up so many gloomy possibilities.

Certainly we will not dwell on potential worst-case scenarios. We will trust the providence of our gracious God to give us what he knows to be good for us. Nonetheless, we cannot forget the reality that, because

15. C. S. Lewis, *The Silver Chair* (New York: Macmillan Publishing Co., 1973), 59–61.

of the fall, our children live in a world with a curse upon it. The good we hope for our children *may* occur. But we can give them no other world to live in than this fallen one. Our children's environment, no matter what their home address is, will be horribly marred by sin and its results. They *will* have great sorrows and struggles, sooner or later. Will they be ready? In Derek Thomas's commentary, *The Storm Breaks: Job Simply Explained*, he notes: "Unlike their counterparts today, Christians of a bygone era prepared themselves for trouble. They expected it. They anticipated the discipline of the cross throughout their earthly lives—until the grave. They understood that pain only dissipates in heaven. The entrance into the kingdom of God is strewn with days of tribulation, some of it intense."[16] In our culture, it's easy to forget that suffering is part of the human condition. Our homes and possessions, our entertainment and our comforts keep us busy and happy, so we have no need to consider suffering at all—unless, of course, it suddenly comes calling on us. As Emily Dickinson wrote of death, "Because I could not stop for Death, he kindly stopped for me."[17] Like death, suffering will come, whether we expect it or not. And when it does, it may be a little late to prepare for it.

Michael Horton's very helpful book, *A Place for Weakness*, provides theology for times of suffering. Horton recommends that we read it *before* we suffer, as a means of preparation. He writes that it's hard to do theology when we are in the middle of a fiery trial. "Understanding who God is, who we are, and God's ways in creation, providence, and redemption—at least as much as Scripture reveals to us—is to the trials of life what preparing for the LSAT is to the practice of law," Horton writes. "Theology is the most serious business. Preparing for this exam is not just a head game or a prerequisite for a temporal vocation, but it's a matter of life and death. It is about our heavenly vocation and its implications for each day here and now. It's about living, and dying, well."[18]

16. Derek Thomas, *The Storm Breaks: Job Simply Explained* (Webster, NY: Evangelical Press, 2005), 11.

17. Emily Dickinson, "Because I could not stop for death," in *101 Great American Poems*, ed. Andrew Carroll, Dover Thrift Editions (Mineola, NY: Dover Publications, 1998), 29.

18. Michael S. Horton, *A Place for Weakness* (Grand Rapids: Zondervan, 2006), 19.

This is, in fact, what I advocate for our children. They will need theology—the thorough knowledge of God as he has revealed himself in Scripture—to live their adult lives well. They will need a hearty biblical worldview when they face the exams that suffering will bring. During their childhood, that relatively carefree phase of their lives, they should be learning theology and learning it well, just as they should study for the math test before the teacher hands it out.

We may not be around to watch our children take their exams. Once they are grown and living on their own, we may be available to coach them when they ask, but we may not be. The nature of their trials may be such that they keep those trials to themselves. Or we may live far away or may no longer live on this earth at all. Amy Carmichael spent a lifetime in India, raising orphan children for the glory of God. She said of the spiritual training of children: "You work for the years you will not see. You work for the Invisible all the time, but you work for the Eternal. So it is all worthwhile."[19] During those years we will not see, the need of our children may be great. We make a way for them to go forward then if, now, we are teaching them truth strong enough to hold them. A wise captain outfits his ship with a sturdy lifeboat at the very outset of the voyage, before any hint of a need for it. So wise parents will supply, during childhood, the "head knowledge" on which, one stormy day, their children's survival may depend.

Why Know

- In our fallen world, suffering *will* come. Learning God's truth well, while we're not suffering, will enable us to endure when we are.
- Learning theology is like studying for exams—when we're tested, we want to be ready.

---

19. Elisabeth Elliot, *A Chance To Die: The Life and Legacy of Amy Carmichael* (Old Tappan, NJ: Fleming H. Revell Co., 1987), 358.

PART TWO

What Our Children Need to Know

CHOOSING OUR BUILDING MATERIALS

Once upon a time there were three little pigs who left home to make their way in the world. They all decided to build houses for themselves. The first little pig chose to build his house of straw. Straw was inexpensive, and a house made of it would be easy to build. The second little pig chose to make his house of sticks. His house might cost a little more, in terms of materials and labor, but he should still have plenty of time and money left to amuse himself as he saw fit.

The third little pig was serious about his house. Unlike his brothers, he wanted a *real* house. He understood that a structure isn't a house because someone says it's a house; it's a house if it can serve as a shelter and as living quarters. How much shelter can straw—or even sticks—provide in a storm? Won't the rain drip through and the cold easily penetrate? Won't the wind tear such "houses" apart—as, in fact, even the wind generated by the breath of a hungry wolf eventually demonstrated? Our third little pig, being serious about his house, had to invest in it. He had to spend time earning money to purchase bricks, and then spend more time building a house with them. But in the end, only one pig had a house that fit the definition of a house. Only that house stood up to the assault of a wolf eager for a ham dinner.

Many belief systems in our day go by the name of "Christian." Many people call themselves "Christians." But just like calling a structure a *house* doesn't make it one, so calling something *Christian* doesn't make it Christian. Only Christ and the apostles he chose get to determine what is truly Christian—or, as they put it, what is the true testimony of the disciples (John 21:24), what is "the pattern of the sound words" (2 Tim. 1:13), what are "the traditions that you were taught" by the apostles "either by . . . spoken word or by . . . letter"(2 Thess. 2:15), what is the "true grace of God" (1 Peter 5:12), and what is "the faith that was once for all delivered to the saints" (Jude 3). There are set and specific truths that comprise the Christian faith, and for something to be *Christian*, it must embrace those truths. Conversely, there are limits and parameters. Teaching and ideas that go beyond what Christ and the apostles laid down as the foundation of the faith are not Christian, no matter what their advocates call them. We want our children to have a true and lasting faith, and so we must build, not with what might be easiest, or with what might cost the least, but with what truly makes Christianity *Christian*.

Christianity is, first of all, a body of truth—to be known, understood, embraced, applied, and passed on. "Spiritual" ideas and feelings, divorced from that body of truth, are not Christian, no matter what those who have them say. Our children must know, first of all, the body of truth taught by Jesus, built upon and communicated by the apostles, and passed down in the church through centuries. Without that body of truth, they do not have Christianity.

Each of the chapters in this section of the book will deal with one or more of Christianity's foundational truth concepts. We will survey some of the big ideas belonging to that concept, some of the basic "bricks" needing to be built into our children's belief systems. We will look at what specific help these beliefs can provide for our children when they face temptation and trial. In some cases, we will consider the *mis*understanding contemporary culture has of these concepts, making it all the more important that our children know the truth. In a few cases, we will take at least a passing glance at child-appropriate ways to begin communicating some of these big ideas to children.

3

God: The Father Almighty, Maker of Heaven and Earth

GOD IS CREATOR

One of the earliest statements of Christian faith, the Apostles' Creed, begins with the statement, "I believe in God the Father Almighty, Maker of heaven and earth." What people believe about how all things came into being has consequences for everything else they think. To believe in the God of the Bible is to believe in a Creator who had a purpose and a goal for his creation and who has remained involved with it, to direct it toward his chosen end. A common view in Western culture holds that all that exists came about by time plus chance. Humans themselves are seen as the result of the right set of conditions at the right time, allowing us to evolve into what we are today. In this belief system, there is no objective standard for right and wrong. What is, is right. Another increasingly common teaching in the West, having migrated from other religious philosophies, is that, while "the Divine" exists, it is not something separate from creation. It is the composite of all that is, so that we ourselves are part of deity. To believe this is to look inside for guidance and for salvation, exactly the opposite of where Christianity teaches us to look.

To know the Creator God of the Bible is to know where we come from and where we're going. It's to have a basic orientation for all of life. It's to have a starting place and the certainty that there is a destination. To understand God as the Creator who made all that exists is to believe in an ultimate reference point. Meaning for all things is found in him. The framers of the Apostles' Creed showed wisdom in beginning with God as Creator. This provides the foundation for all else we must believe to have a biblical faith. As J. I. Packer writes in *A Concise Theology*, "Knowing that God created the world around us, and ourselves as part of it, is basic to true religion. . . . Realizing our moment-by-moment dependence on God the Creator for our very existence makes it appropriate to live lives of devotion, commitment, gratitude, and loyalty toward him, and scandalous not to. Godliness starts here, with God the sovereign Creator as the first focus of our thoughts."[1]

The concept of God as Creator is one of the easiest and most natural places to begin in teaching young children about God. God has given children an inherent fascination with everything around them. Since a basic principle of teaching anything is to use the familiar to teach the unfamiliar, it will be perfectly natural, as your child makes each new discovery of creation's wonders, to point out that it is God who made this thing; look at how wisely and well he has made it.

Things to Know

- God is the Creator of all that is.
- Understanding that God is the Creator provides the foundation for understanding every other aspect of life.

GOD IS ONE GOD, EXISTING IN THREE PERSONS

After the initial statement of belief in "God the Father Almighty, Maker of heaven and earth," the Apostles' Creed goes on to spell out belief in the other two persons of the Trinity. This sets Christianity apart from other religions—even monotheistic ones—and cults. Orthodox Christianity, like Judaism and Islam, believes in one true and living God; unlike those religions, Christianity teaches that the one God exists in three persons. Each person is distinct and separate from the other two, and the three persons can have communication and fellowship with each other. Yet they are not three Gods, but one.

Older children may be interested to know that nowhere in the Bible does it say that God is one God in three persons. Yet it is the clear

1. J. I. Packer, *A Concise Theology* (Wheaton, IL: Tyndale House Publishers, 1993), 22.

teaching of Scripture. You can remind them of *the* big moral issue of so many Old Testament stories: idolatry. From the building of the golden calf through the fall of Jerusalem, God's people continually tried to worship God *and*. The prophets warned and threatened for centuries, to no avail, as the people tried to cling to idols along with God. You can direct your children to God's words in Deuteronomy 6:4, words memorized early in life by every Jewish child: "Hear, O Israel: The LORD our God, the LORD is one." Then you can point out what it would have been like to have been Jesus' disciples, Jewish men who had grown up saying those very words every day, but who watched Jesus do one thing after another that only God could do, until they understood that Jesus—who spoke to God his Father—was truly God. Then you can point them to Jesus' words in his final discourse with them (John 14–17), where he promises to send "another Helper" (14:6), who would be in them all and who would be with them always. Who can be in all places at one time, forever, if he is not God?

As for how to explain how one Being can exist in three persons, there simply is no adequate comparison or illustration to make. We must begin our earliest teaching of our children with mystery. God is unique. It isn't that there are three different forms of God, manifesting themselves according to the need of the moment (like H_2O in water, steam, and ice). There are three separate persons in one, and only one, God.

Things to Know
- There is only one God.
- God exists in three persons: Father, Son, and Holy Spirit.
- The Trinity is too mysterious for our finite minds to fully comprehend.

GOD IS TRANSCENDENT

A discussion of the Trinity invariably leads to the realization that we will never understand God completely. Our children need to know there are things we can know and understand about God, but there are many things about him that are too big for even the best minds. While God made all that exists and cares about it, he is outside of and beyond his creation. As Solomon put it in his prayer at the temple's dedication, "But will God indeed dwell on the earth? Behold, heaven and the highest heaven cannot contain you" (1 Kings 8:27). If the universe is too small to contain God, then a creature in that universe, even one made in the image of God, cannot grasp all that God is. Modern religious man never questions his own assumptions about God. He has opinions, feelings, and ideas about God that seem right to him, so he chooses to believe them. The person who doesn't understand the transcendence of God does not realize he needs God to reveal himself, or he cannot know him. Modern men and women are all too often like those whom God rebukes in Psalm 50:21 by saying, "You thought that I was one like yourself." It is in appreciating the transcendence of God that we become aware of the value of Scripture. In it, the God we could never know on our own tells us something of what he is like.

From the beginning, we must get comfortable with telling our children, "God is so much greater than we are that we can't always understand him." You may be able to help them with this sense of mystery by encouraging them to consider their pet's view of them. The family dog or cat may like it when your child pets it, may run to your child eager for its food, and may come when your child calls. But the pet has no idea of what your child is doing when he takes off his play clothes and puts on his pajamas. The dog or cat has no concept of reading a book or doing homework. These are incomprehensible mysteries your child's pet just has to live with. Yet the distance between the great and infinite God and his finite creatures is far greater than the distance between your child and his pet.

Accepting the mystery of God may not completely satisfy our children's curiosity, but it provides the beginnings of lifelong comfort. People believe God owes them explanations for things that happen. How many times have we heard: "Why me?" "Why would God allow that?" "Why do bad things happen to good people?" When an explanation is not forthcoming, people vengefully turn their backs on God, refusing to believe in a Divine Being who doesn't do things the way they think he should. If our children accept that God, by definition, is greater than they are, they can rest at peace when they do not understand all that he does or his reasons for doing it.

Things to Know

- God is outside creation.
- God is greater than anything he has created.
- God is far greater than our minds can grasp.

GOD IS A SPIRIT

I find that even older children are often surprised to consider that God is a Spirit and does not have a body. No doubt this is because Scripture so often refers to body parts when it speaks of God. His eyes see all that men do (Ps. 11:4); his ears hear the cry of the righteous (Ps. 34:15); he acts on behalf of his people with an outstretched arm (Deut. 5:15); his hand is on all who seek him to do them good (Ezra 8:22); and his mouth speaks truth and makes promises to his people (2 Chron. 6:4; 36:22). Children enjoy new words, especially if they're big ones. Teach your children *anthropomorphism*, the attributing of human characteristics to something (in this case *someone*) that is not human. God uses anthropomorphism when he refers to his hands, his arm, his eyes, his ears. He speaks of what he can do in terms easy for us to understand, so he describes himself as having a body when he does not. When Jesus came to live among us, he took to himself a human body and soul. In fact, one of the reasons the Son of God had to become flesh was so that he would have a body and could die in the place of his people.

Things to Know

- God is Spirit. He has no body.
- The Bible speaks of God's hands, eyes, etc., to help us understand he acts, he sees, etc.

GOD IS OMNIPRESENT

Other spirit beings exist—angels and demons, for example—but God alone is a Spirit who is in all places at the same time. "Am I a God at hand, declares the LORD, and not a God far away? Can a man hide himself in secret places so that I cannot see him? declares the LORD. Do I not fill heaven and earth? declares the LORD" (Jer. 23:23–24). God's people, who know that their God possesses all power and all wisdom and who know that he cares for them so much that he gave his Son for their salvation, have the assurance that this God is always with them. When recess rolls around and a kindergartner's best friend has stayed home sick, that lonely kindergartner can know she's not alone; God is right there with her on the playground. In hospital rooms, for her own treatment or watching by the bed of a loved one, in places of ministry where she feels inadequate, in times of work or school stress, in war, in natural disaster—anywhere your child might one day find herself, and however cut off she may feel from human help—she can know God is there with her. And more—she can count on an omnipresent God to be with those she loves when they have a need she cannot meet.

The fact of an omnipresent God provides immeasurable comfort through all scenes and stages of life. At the same time, it carries with it the threat of rousing God's displeasure. While we can hide our misdeeds from other humans, we can hide nothing from God. We can never get off alone by ourselves to do something we want no one to see, for God will be there, and he will see it. In the Bible I've owned the longest, next to Psalm 90:8 ("You have set our iniquities before you, our secret sins in the light of your presence"), I once wrote these words, from a source I no longer remember: "Life becomes an awesome business when you realize that you spend every moment of your life in the sight and company of an omniscient, omnipresent Creator." Children in their teens or in their adult years who have grown up in the awareness of God's omnipresence will have a built-in safeguard from temptations that could destroy them.

On the other hand, sometimes the awareness that God sees every sin brings comfort. Those are all the times when evil seems to triumph or when the innocent suffer at the hands of merciless oppressors. More likely than not, your children will experience some version of such injustice. They will be cheated out of something that was their own, or they will be injured in some way, and the one who caused the injury will refuse to take responsibility for it. They may be physically assaulted or have dealings with legal systems that are either flawed or deliberately corrupt. If they don't experience these things themselves, they will surely witness them in the lives of others and in the daily news. God, who is in all places at all times, is a witness to every sin and every injustice and, while human courts fail, God's justice does not. Those who suffer according to the will of God are free to "entrust their souls to a faithful Creator" (1 Peter 4:19) for this very reason: God has seen the evil human actions that have caused the suffering, and he will punish every one.

The story of Jonah, beloved by children, provides lessons in what God's omnipresence can mean to a believer. Read the whole story with your children (all four short chapters), and have them list the places Jonah was where God was also present. Have them tell you when Jonah would have been glad to have God with him and when he would like to have been out of God's presence. Encourage your child to name some specific instances when people today would be glad to know that God is with them, as well as times they might be disturbed to think that God is where they are right now.

When you discuss your child's daily experiences with him, remind him to consider that God was with him at different times when he felt troubled. The presence of God didn't make the unpleasant circumstances go away, but it should provide the comfort of knowing that God was aware of those circumstances. He could have changed them, and, if he didn't, it was because God knew those very circumstances to be, somehow, for the best. And God was with your child to be sure he would have what he needed to make it through the difficult situation.

Things to Know

- God is in all places at all times.
- God sees all things that take place.
- God will call every action to judgment at the right time.

GOD IS OMNISCIENT

It can stagger our little minds to consider all that God holds in his. Since God is omnipresent, he must be aware of all that happens anywhere in the universe at any time. But God knows more than that. He knows what every rational being is thinking, feeling, or planning at any given moment. He knows all that happened, all that was thought, all that was felt, and all that was planned at any and every moment of the past. He knows all that will happen, and all that will be thought, felt, and planned at every moment in the future. He knows every fact and every property related to every created thing, the billions of facts that all humanity combined know as well as the billions more that remain unknown to man. And more—God knows all contingencies. God knows that you went to the store at 10 a.m. yesterday, but he also knows every "what would have happened" for every other thing you could have done besides going to the store yesterday, and he knows that information regarding every single incident that occurred at 10 a.m. yesterday!

As your child goes through life, what he knows of God will prove a tremendous comfort to him if God is his God. One of the things he should know is that God possesses all knowledge. When your child faces a decision or fears an unknown future, he can trust that the God who has promised to lead him knows all that he does not know. In times of strained relationships, when others have misunderstood or wrongly judged him, your child can rest in the assurance that God—whose opinion matters most—knows his heart. Even the assurance that God knows all our sin brings comfort. Isn't it true that if even our dearest loved ones knew what we were *really* like they would turn from us in disgust? But God knows his people inside out. Your child can rejoice in the love of God who knows the very worst about him—and who goes on loving. God will never discover something about your child that will cause him to cast him off. God already knows it all.

You can get your child to begin to consider what it means for God to know everything by asking her to tell you some of the things she *doesn't* know. "What will the weather be like on your birthday?" "What is your best friend doing right now?" "What word am I thinking of?" "How many stars are there (exact number, please)?" "What are the names of every person who was alive on the earth five-hundred years ago today?" None of this is difficult for God. He knows all. You can help your child to practice living in the awareness of God's unlimited knowledge by reminding her, when good things happen to her, "Did God know you would like that?" Likewise, when things aren't going her way, "Does God know what you would rather have? Does God know what's best? Can you trust him to choose this for you instead?"

When we give our children vocabulary, we familiarize them with the concepts the words represent. You can demonstrate how words are like Lego bricks; you can take them apart and reassemble the pieces with other parts to make something different. School-age children probably know the terms *carnivore* (meat-eater) and *herbivore* (plant-eater). Explain to them that an *omnivore* eats all things, plants or meat. Bears, skunks, and humans are omnivores. Then use *omni* and add it to *present*, meaning *here*, to get *all-present* or *present in all places*. Add *omni* to *scient* (related to *science* and meaning *knowing*), and you have *omniscient, all-knowing*. You can also do this with *potent*, a word for *strong*. *Omnipotent* means *all-powerful*. People avoid theological words in general, and especially with children. But theological words have such wealth of meaning! So, instead, let's use them and make sure to teach their meanings to our children.

Things to Know

- God knows everything—everything that is, that has been, that will be, that could be.

GOD POSSESSES ALL WISDOM

Infinite wisdom requires infinite knowledge, for wisdom knows the best thing possible and knows the best possible way to attain it. I knew a boy once who lived in foster care. He had seen his father, who was now in jail, murder his mother. When he heard me say that God possesses all wisdom, he laughed scornfully and said, "God sees all the stuff that goes on and lets it happen, and you call that *wise?*"

That boy wasn't alone in his thinking. Many people in our time maintain that they cannot believe in the existence of God because of all the ugly things that happen in our world. If there was a God, they say, he would stop those things from happening. Others, who profess faith, experience some deep and terrible trauma, and then cannot recover from the shock. They thought God was wise and in control, and then this thing occurred. They must have been mistaken, they conclude.

As we teach our children the infinite, perfect wisdom of God, we need to also teach them the goal that God, in his wisdom, pursues. The Bible tells us that God's ultimate goal is his own glory (Hab. 2:14). This makes perfect sense, because all things were created to give glory to God (Rom. 11:36). God receiving glory, therefore, results in the highest possible good for all creation. Having a sinful nature due to the fall, we wrongly place ourselves at the center of the universe and expect that the goal of all things is the comfort and happiness of human beings. We assume that God must have this same standard so, when things happen that make us feel miserable and *un*comfortable, it shakes our faith in the wisdom of a Divine Being. Our children will grow strong if they grow up understanding the nature of God's wisdom. They will rest on the assurance that his goal is the demonstration of his own glory, that he is always steadily working to accomplish that goal by the best possible means, and that displaying his glory will prove to be the highest good for the universe and for us, his people.

At times, our children may receive or may witness a blow so severe that it will seem impossible to believe that, somehow, this must be for God's glory. At those times, our children can look to the cross, where, Paul tells us, we see the most brilliant display of God's wisdom (1 Cor. 1:21–24). Had we stood in John's shoes at the foot of the cross on that Friday when God's Son, the Messiah, hung suffering, after hours of torture at the hands of his enemies, we would not have thought we were seeing the wisdom and power of God on display. We would have found it hard to see how God could receive glory from this. And yet, Jesus told his disciples, once he had risen, that these things *had* to be this way (Luke 24:25–26). It was precisely through this unspeakable horror of a crucified Messiah that God accomplished his wise plan of bringing glory to himself by saving sinners and overthrowing his enemies. More than only showing them an example of God's wisdom where they wouldn't naturally expect it, the cross can also encourage our children to trust themselves to God's wisdom when they suffer and cannot imagine why. Whatever the reason for their suffering is, they can know that it is *not* because God is unconcerned. At the cross, they will find the assurance that God cares deeply for his children, for there they see God the Son absorbing pain greater than any they will ever know—precisely because God *does* love and care about them.

Things to Know

- God possesses all wisdom.
- He has the best possible goal for all things—his own glory—and uses the best possible means to attain that goal.

GOD IS OMNIPOTENT

God told Jeremiah to buy a field in Anathoth, near Jerusalem. This made no sense. The army of the world's most powerful king, Nebuchadnezzar, stood outside the city gates, and Jerusalem lay under siege. God had promised that Jerusalem would fall and that God's people would be driven from the land for their failure to keep his covenant. Jeremiah himself was in prison for his faithful proclamation of this gloomy news from God. But God had also promised that, after a time of exile, he would bring his people back to their land. God's explanation to Jeremiah was this: "Behold, I am the LORD, the God of all flesh. Is anything too hard for me" (Jer. 32:27)? The third major *omni* word concerning God that we can give our children is this one: *omnipotent*, or *all-powerful*. When our children grasp the doctrine of God's omnipotence, they have the comforting certainty that all God has promised concerning them, his people, and his universe will come to pass. If he has promised that, one day, they will be without sin, they will be. If he has promised that they will grow ever more like Christ, they will. If he has promised to preserve his church and bring it, at last, triumphant to heaven, he will do it. If he has promised that all things will work together for good to those who love him, this will be the case, both in the lives of our children and in the lives of those they love when they number among "those who are called according to his purpose" (Rom. 8:28). Nothing can prevent God from fulfilling all his promises because he has more power than any obstacle that could arise.

The doctrine of God's omnipotence will also bring comfort when our children face unthinkable situations they are helpless to change. *God* can change those situations. He very well may not; suffering is often the path he chooses for his children, wanting their holiness more than their happiness. But when our children face the terrible, they can pray, knowing the One to whom they pray has the power to do what they ask. If he doesn't give them what they ask for, they can know that it's not because he *cannot*; for his own wise purposes, he has chosen not to. They can rest in the assurance that what they face is part of his wise plan for them; they face, not a horror God cannot overcome, but his will for them in this time. Job learned this in the midst of enormous anguish. God never told Job *why* he didn't relieve his sufferings or even why he had chosen for Job to endure them. Instead, God reminded Job of his great power and wisdom so he would realize that he could trust what God did with him, whether or not he saw the reason. "I know that you can do all things, and that no purpose of yours can be thwarted," Job told God at the end of it all (Job 42:2).

Even when God does not use his great might to change their circumstances, our children can still find strength to face them in knowing his omnipotence. God has promised to be with his people always, making all his great power available to fortify them when they face temptation and trial. He shares all that he is with his children, for their good and his glory. Isaiah 40 lists a series of illustrations of God's strength and greatness, drawn from what he has created and how he cares for it. The chapter ends by reminding God's discouraged people that he doesn't grow tired or faint himself, and he will supply his people with power when they feel weary and exhausted. He promises that "they who wait for the LORD shall renew their strength; they shall mount up with wings like eagles; they shall run and not be weary; they shall walk and not faint" (Isa. 40:31). When our children face challenges that seem far too big for them, they can know that God's power will supply what they lack. Before Jesus handed off to his disciples the staggering task of taking the gospel into the entire world, he assured them, "All authority in heaven and on earth has been given to me." After he explained their task, he added, "And behold, I am with you always, to the end of the age" (Matt. 28:18–20).

One child-appropriate and enjoyable way to introduce the topic of God's greatness and power to children is to work through Isaiah 40:12–18 together. Encourage children to move water from one container to another by handfuls, counting how many handfuls it took; then encourage them to name bodies of water they can remember (specific seas, oceans, and rivers). Have them spread their fingers to make a span and measure a wall of the room with it. Consider with them that God "measured the waters" (every drop, in all those bodies of water you named) "in the hollow of his hand and marked off the heavens with a span" (Isa. 40:12a). Use measuring cups to see how much sand is in a container, and use a scale to weigh it and then to weigh some rocks. Name mountains you can think of. Point out that God "enclosed the dust of the earth in a measure" (all of it!) "and weighed the mountains" (all of them!) "in scales and the hills in a balance" (Isa. 40:12b). Scatter a little dust on the same scale and see if the weight of it registers at all. Fill a bucket with water and add one more drop. Together, name all the nations you can think of. Then read verse 15: "Behold, the nations are like a drop from a bucket, and are accounted as the dust on the scales."

There are those who would say that wanting to rely on someone greater, stronger, and wiser than we are demonstrates immaturity, even cowardice. They would insist that, like Hemingway's fisherman in *The Old Man and the Sea*, our worth is seen in how we go on fighting, against all odds, in a perverse environment, depending on nothing but ourselves and our own resources. At one point, just in case it might help, Hemingway's fisherman prays for help in bringing in the great marlin he had harpooned. "With his prayers said, and feeling much better, but suffering exactly as much, and perhaps a little more," the old man continues his long ordeal, with Hemingway pointing out again and again how much he suffered, how brave he was in the face of it, and how he endured with no help at all from anyone.[2]

To deny oneself the help and comfort available in an omnipotent, omniscient Creator in exchange for the delusion of self-reliance—what folly! To insist that no being exists who is wiser or stronger than we are—what arrogance! But, on the other hand, what tragedy to comfort ourselves with ideas of a fantasy God we've made up, who doesn't exist at all. We can help to guard our children from all these things when we teach them, early and well, who God is as he has revealed himself in his Word.

Things to Know

- God possesses all power.
- Nothing can keep God from carrying out his plans.
- God's omnipotence should ultimately be a comfort to us.

2. Ernest Hemingway, *The Old Man and the Sea* (New York: Scribner, 2003), 65.

4

God: As He Is, Not God as We Want Him to Be

GOD IS SOVEREIGN

The sad reality concerning the essential truth of the sovereignty of God is that it has become the minority report in the contemporary American church. People associate God's sovereignty with predestination in salvation, which they don't like. God wouldn't really choose some people, and not others, to save, would he? That's not fair!

Predestination in salvation is only one small facet of God's attribute of sovereignty. And the sovereignty of God, his absolute reign, is taught clearly through the whole Bible, from Genesis 1 through Revelation 22. God rules his universe (Ps. 103:19). He made it, and he does with it as he chooses. God always accomplishes all his purposes, and nothing can thwart them (Dan. 4:34–35). By definition, God *must* be sovereign. Even dictionary.com gives the first definition of *God* as "the one Supreme Being, the creator and ruler of the universe." Since *supreme* means greater and higher than all others, there can be only one Supreme Being. The Supreme Being has the authority and the power to command everything else. If God is God, he commands all aspects of all things, in every nook and corner of his universe. This is what we mean by *sovereignty*. *Sovereign* as an adjective is defined as "having supreme rank, power, or authority," and, as a noun, it is defined as "a person who has supreme power or authority." By definition, then, God, the Supreme Being, must be sovereign. Paul describes God as being the one "who works *all things* according to the counsel of his will" (Eph. 1:11). He is over everything, including every human and his or her destiny. God commands, and everyone and everything else obey. Nothing can go off on its own, ignoring the will of this Ruler. He is sovereign.

The doctrine of the sovereignty of God comforts like no other doctrine. It teaches our children that all God's good, loving, holy purposes, for us and for his creation, will come to pass. It teaches them that nothing can happen outside of God's control. If something that seems bad to them occurs, it is not because God was helpless to prevent it. Rather, its ultimate cause is the wise purpose of a good God. There are no accidents, no evil forces beyond God's power to rein them in. The most unsettling things our children will ever encounter fit somewhere into the will of God and have a part in accomplishing the purposes he has determined.

God is sovereign in his creation. He created it, he sustains it, and he still actively directs it. When an unexpected pregnancy takes our adult daughter by surprise, she can know that God created this child at this time for these parents because such was his wise will. Even if the child develops abnormally and has a disease or birth defect, God the sovereign Creator, who knows the best goals and the best means for attaining those goals, has ordained even this. Moses complained that he had no particular gifts as a public speaker for confronting Pharaoh and leading God's people. "Then the Lord said to him, 'Who has made man's mouth? Who makes him mute, or deaf, or seeing, or blind? Is it not I, the Lord?'" (Ex. 4:11). When powerful forces of nature rise up to disturb our children's peace—hurricanes, tornadoes, or earthquakes—God has sovereignly ordained them. He says through one prophet, "Does disaster come to a city, unless the Lord has done it?" (Amos 3:6) Through another, he says, "I form light and create darkness, I make well-being and create calamity, I am the Lord, who does all these things" (Isa. 45:7). When your children firmly believe in God's sovereignty, they can know why upheavals that touch their lives occur—God commands them to. They will probably not see his reasons, but they can know he has reasons, and they are wise ones. God is accomplishing a good purpose. This perspective makes all the difference between hope and despair. We do our children a world of good when we teach them to see the entire universe as under the rule of a wise, good, and *sovereign* God.

God is sovereign in his providence. "God's providence," the *Shorter Catechism* teaches us, "is His completely holy, wise, and powerful preserving and governing every creature and every action."[1] God directs what happens, when it happens, and to whom it happens. When our children are among "those who love God," they have the promise that, for them, God has ordained that "all things work together for good" (Rom. 8:28). The providence of God can help when our children agonize over decisions. We face far more choices than our parents and our grandparents did, and our children will face even more. The very number of choices can paralyze people from choosing anything at all. What if I make the wrong choice? What if I choose the wrong school, career, location, job, or spouse? As believers in the sovereignty of God, our children do not need to anxiously second-guess their every decision for fear that they missed God's best for them. They cannot sabotage God's plans for them. *He* is sovereign; they are not. As answer 1 of The Heidelberg Catechism assures:

> He also watches over me in such a way
> that not a hair can fall from my head
> without the will of my Father in heaven;
> in fact, all things must work together for my salvation.[2]

In writing of the cloud that led Israel through the wilderness by day and the pillar of fire that led them by night, Matthew Henry states that, in these last days when Christ has appeared and the gospel has been proclaimed, we should no longer expect such physically manifested guidance as the Israelites enjoyed. Still, Henry says of God's people, "There is a particular providence conversant about all their affairs, to direct and overrule them for the best."[3] To know the sovereignty of God

1. Douglas Kelly and Philip Rollinson, *The Westminster Shorter Catechism in Modern English* (Phillipsburg, NJ: Presbyterian and Reformed Publishing Company, 1986), 6.

2. Faith Alive Christian Resources, *The Heidelberg Catechism: 450th Anniversary Edition* (Faith Alive Christian Resources, 2013), 8.

3. Matthew Henry, *Commentary on the Whole Bible Volume 1* (Grand Rapids: Christian Classics Ethereal Library), http://www.ccel.org/ccel/henry/mhc1.i.html.

is to know that a loving Father sends every providence. It is to possess peace that will last a lifetime.

God is sovereign over all things, and that includes salvation. When our Christian children understand this, that understanding will produce in them at least two godly responses. First, it will cause them to give all the glory to God for all they have that is most important. God has done everything concerning their salvation. Neither they, nor anyone else, helped God save them. God crafted the plan of salvation, provided the Savior, and applied salvation to them by the Holy Spirit. God chose them; he ordered their circumstances so that they would hear the gospel; he caused them to be born again, and he opened their understanding so the gospel would make sense to them. He convicted them of sin and worked repentance in them, and he gave them the faith to trust in Christ. He gave the Holy Spirit to live in them, and, through that Spirit, he gives them the power to deny sin and to grow in Christlike character. God has done everything to save them, and they can claim no credit for themselves. Secondly, an awareness of God's sovereignty in salvation will give our children the peace of knowing that, as God has done everything so far for their salvation, so he will do everything to bring them, finally, home to live in his presence in heaven forever. Every time the apostles make a statement such as "the God of all grace, who has called you to his eternal glory in Christ, will himself restore, confirm, strengthen, and establish you" (1 Peter 5:10) or "and I am sure of this, that he who began a good work in you will bring it to completion at the day of Jesus Christ" (Phil. 1:6), they attest to their confidence in God's sovereignty in salvation. Your children may have days when they feel God cannot possibly forgive them for the sin they just committed or for a recurring sin they have committed yet again. Yet they can know that salvation is *all* of God. God knew when he chose them exactly which sins they would commit, when, and how often. He chose them *in spite* of their moral character, not because of it. He saves them because salvation is from the Lord, not from those who are saved. Salvation by grace is all about God, able and willing to save; we can in no way save ourselves, nor can we, by our sins and shortcomings, undo his work in us. Jesus, speaking of those who believe in him and calling them his sheep, said, "They will never perish, and no one will snatch them out of my hand. My Father, who has given them to me, is greater than all," (again, he is supreme; there is none greater, not even our sin) "and no one is able to snatch them out of the Father's hand" (John 10:28–29).

Nothing we can give our children will prove a support during trial like the certainty of God's sovereignty. Children naturally love stories, and some specific Bible stories bring home God's sovereignty in concrete ways. Tell them the story of Joseph, who came to see that his many miserable circumstances were sent by God to accomplish his good purposes. The book of Jonah, already mentioned as a convincing illustration of God's omniscience, also demonstrates the sovereignty of God. As you read through it with your children, list all the creatures that did God's bidding, from hardened sailors to a tiny worm. In Job's sad story, even Satan had to have God's permission before seeking to tempt Job through affliction. God made the sun and moon stand still for Joshua (Josh. 10:1–15); he caused the king of Assyria to withdraw from his siege of Jerusalem (2 Kings 19); he sent Abigail to prevent David from taking vengeance on Nabal (1 Sam. 25).

Esther is another story that demonstrates God's sovereignty, yet without directly crediting God's work behind the scenes. Once children know that the book of Esther never mentions God, they will enjoy going on a God-hunt through its pages. How many demonstrations of God's wise providence can they find in the story's "it just so happened" incidents?

The Bible's conversion stories too, so familiar we may fail to notice them, illustrate God's commitment to bring specific individuals to himself. In the Gospels, people meet Jesus, face to face. Jesus stops to look up under Zacchaeus's tree (Luke 19:1–10) and rests at a well just when a Samaritan woman is coming for water (John 4:4–42). In the book of Acts, individual conversions occur. The Ethiopian is reading a prophecy about Jesus' dying for sin just when Philip comes to ask if he understands what he's reading (Acts 8:26–40), and when Paul speaks at a prayer meeting, God opens Lydia's heart to believe the gospel (Acts 16:13–15).

In all these conversion examples, the backstories include all kinds of circumstances God had to orchestrate to bring these things to pass.

The "down side" to the sovereignty of God, from the perspective of sinful human beings, is that if God rules, we don't. Sinners by nature, we want our way, not God's. We are like the citizens in the parable Jesus told, complaining about the nobleman who went on a journey and would return. "But his citizens hated him . . . , saying, 'We do not want this man to reign over us' " (Luke 19:14). Our culture insists that we think of ourselves first; anything else is unhealthy. Our culture demands that we make our own choices and rule our own lives. It wants us to sing with Frank Sinatra that we did it our way. Anything else is for the weak. So human beings forfeit the wonderful comfort they could have in knowing God rules in order to hang on to the illusion that *they're* in control and no one tells *them* what to do. Our call as parents and teachers is to make sure our children understand that, to believe in the God of the Bible, they must believe in a God who rules over all.

Things to Know

- God is the highest ruler over all.
- God rules his creation. It all does his will.
- God rules in providence (all the ordinary—and extraordinary— things that happen every day).
- God rules in salvation. He does everything that needs done to save every one of the people he has chosen.

GOD IS HOLY

In today's world, God's holiness isn't any more popular than is his sovereignty. People rejoice in a God who has power and who can do things they want to have done. They find comfort in a God who loves them and always watches out for them, someone they can turn to in desperate moments of need. They like having a God who has basically the same likes and dislikes as they do, who values what they value and wants what they want. But holiness is old-fashioned. It's what Puritans in funny-looking clothes believed about God. Ideas of holiness, our contemporaries would say, result in self-righteous, hateful attitudes toward those who have different standards. They would say that those who claim holiness for God make him out to be critical, overly concerned about rules, and mean enough to send people to hell. Most contemporary Westerners who still claim to believe in God have no room for a God who is holy.

By the Bible's terms, though, holiness is basic to the character of God. Our children can only believe in the God of the Bible if they understand and embrace God's holiness. The seraphim who stand always in God's presence claim holiness as God's defining characteristic. "Holy, holy, holy is the LORD of hosts; the whole earth is full of his glory (Isa. 6:3). "Holy, holy, holy is the Lord God Almighty, who was and is and is to come" (Rev. 4:8). Even as great a religious leader as Moses was told to take off his shoes in the presence of God, "for the place on which you are standing is holy ground" (Ex. 3:5).

When we read or tell Bible stories to children, we struggle with the temptation to omit stories like the one of the ground opening to swallow Korah and his companions for their rebellion, or the ones about God striking Uzzah dead for touching the ark, and Ananias and Sapphira for telling a lie. These stories, though, present an aspect of God our children must know. We can always remind them that God, in his grace, has provided a way for us to be forgiven, but God's forgiveness has no meaning when divorced from God's holiness. As we tell children these stories, we want to be sure to point out that God has not changed. He is as holy now as he was then, and sin offends him just as greatly.

In that sense, therefore, the holiness of God is not the most comforting of his attributes to consider. Even those of us who have been cleansed by the blood of Christ and have been given new hearts to love righteousness and the law of God still sin multiple times daily. The holiness of God is so blistering white, a purity from all moral defect, that it threatens to undo us completely when we stop to consider it. Isaiah, a righteous man by human standards, cried out in terror in the presence of a holy God (Isa. 6:5). Almost every time a human in the Bible encounters even a mere angel—not God, yet a being who represents the holy God and comes from him—the human responds in terror, often falling to the ground as though dead. In almost every case, the first instruction an angel gives upon appearing is some form of "Don't be afraid." By nature sinners, we are, by nature, terrified when we reflect on the One who is perfectly holy. It's much more comfortable to forget the holiness of God, and it is this self-induced amnesia that permits modern men and women to live in such blatant disregard of God's righteous standards.

There is a gladness, though, in being what we were created to be, in living as we were made to live. God has provided forgiveness for us in Christ, so that we no longer need to wail, as Isaiah did, "Woe is me! For I am lost!" Yet even those who are forgiven are required by this holy God to live holy lives. The apostle Peter, who at one point fell down before Jesus, crying, "Depart from me, for I am a sinful man, O Lord" (Luke 5:8), later wrote to fellow Christians, "But as he who called you is holy, you also be holy in all your conduct" (1 Peter 1:15). God sent his Son to save from *sin*, not just from its punishment. He calls us to holiness, then gives his Spirit to make us able to attain holiness (no, not perfectly in this life, but in a real measure). In living holy lives, your children will find the comfort of resembling the Father who created and redeemed them. They will know the joy of living as they were created to live. And a first step to the motivation of a holy life is knowing this truth: "Holy, holy, holy is the Lord God Almighty."

Comfort comes, too, in knowing that the God who possesses all power and all authority is also a holy God. God will not use his mighty strength to work wickedness or to devastate his creation. He will not rule in such a way that he schemes evil against his subjects. Everything about our great and sovereign God is holy. He plans, desires, and pursues only what is righteous and morally good. Examples abound of earthly rulers who seek their own gain at the expense of those they rule, or who use their authority to attain unrighteous ends. Older children may be able to tell you what they've learned of such rulers from their history studies or from current events. Remind them that the highest ruler over them all, though, is holy. He rules in absolute righteousness and will, one day, bring to an end every rule of evil. Our children may live under unjust rulers. They may be the victims of rulers who oppress their subjects or who persecute them for their beliefs. The sure knowledge that the Most High is holy will provide a firm foundation for their faith in such times.

Things to Know

- God is holy. He is perfectly good and righteous.
- God plans, desires, and pursues only what is righteous and morally good.
- God requires holiness from his people.

GOD IS THE JUST JUDGE

God's justice goes hand in hand with his holiness. Because God is holy, he maintains standards of righteousness in his universe. He gives laws and, because he is righteous, the laws result in good and in well-being for his creation. God requires his moral, rational creatures to keep the laws he gives. Because he is righteous, when his creatures disregard his laws, he judges and punishes them. If, as the highest ruler in the universe, God allowed unrighteousness to go unpunished, his own holiness would be flawed. Imagine a judge who, after a criminal had been convicted of a crime, blew off the offense, saying, "I'm just going to let it go this time." He would be despised by all as an unjust judge.

As modern man does not wish to be ruled, so he does not wish to be judged. He wants to continue in his delusion that any reasonable God would accept him as he is. Modern man scoffs at the thought of a judgment day or of hell—bogeymen, left over from the Dark Ages. Here again, though, if we would be faithful to teach our children *Christian* doctrine and the content of the Bible, we must teach them that God will judge everyone some day. We teach them that he has provided, in Christ, a way to stand in that judgment. At the same time, we make sure they realize that there will be no way to stand other than that one way. Refusal to bow the knee to Christ in repentance and humble faith means choosing to face God's judgment all alone.

God's holiness and justice constitute part of the reason for a biblical fear of God. As modern people, we don't care for fear either. Love for God—sure. Wanting to please him because he's been good to us—okay. Fear, however, seems unworthy to us; yet, from one end of the Bible to the other, God expects his people to fear him. When God first made his covenant with Israel, he appeared on Sinai in cloud, smoke, and lightning. Trumpet and thunder blasted, and the mountain shook. Moses explained that all this was so "that the fear of him may be before you, that you may not sin" (Ex. 20:20). In John's visions of heaven and of the end of history, he saw the triumphant servants of God singing, "Who will not fear, O Lord, and glorify your name? For you alone are holy" (Rev. 15:4). A healthy fear of God, the holy Judge of all, will help to hold our children back when they are tempted to do what they know is wrong. It will help them to stand firm for the righteousness that God loves.

Have your children give examples of injustice or unfairness they have experienced, perhaps at school or when they were playing sports. Consider how Jesus was mistreated and how, at the time, his persecutors seemed to get away with it. Explain how human justice often fails. Evil against others may occur in secret and never come to light in this lifetime. Wicked men may hold so much power that other people cannot bring them to justice. God's judgment comes as a profound comfort in those times. If our children ever find themselves facing the failure of human justice, they can know that all evildoers will one day face God, the Judge of all. Because there is a just and holy God, justice will triumph in the universe.

Things to Know

- God gives laws to humans.
- God will judge all men by his holy laws.

GOD IS GOOD AND GOD IS LOVE

The apostle James writes, "Every good gift and every perfect gift is from above, coming down from the Father of lights" (James 1:17). Whatever we have that we enjoy has, as its source, the goodness of God. Whether the beauty of a sunset or the eyes with which to see it, the delight of chocolate gelato or the coziness of a warm bed on a cold night, the comfort of family or the ability to breathe—all flow out of God's goodness. God is good, and he delights to do good. He bestows gifts with lavish abandon on people who do not deserve them and who, usually, fail to thank him for them. He created a world full of riches and created our bodies and souls so they could appreciate those riches. He sustains that world and us in it, day by day and moment by moment. When we complain about our circumstances, it's because we're comparing them with the circumstances of others, who seem to enjoy gifts we have not received. Our perspective is off because we compare what we have with what others have, rather than comparing what we have with what we deserve. As sinners by nature, we are rebels against God. We fail to thank him for what we have, then complain that we don't have more. Whatever we have is a gift that God did not owe us and that he would have been just to withhold.

God is good, and we do our children a great service by training them to see that fun days with friends, new pajamas, and chocolate chip cookies are all gifts from God. When you see your children enjoying some good gift, get in the habit of asking them, "Who gives us (whatever it is)? Why does he give us these things?" Because God is good, they will be able to bring to him all their concerns, for the people they care about as well as for themselves. God has not promised to give them everything they think they need to be happy; but he is good, and he delights to do good, so they can ask, knowing that if he denies what they see as a good thing, it's never from stinginess or unconcern, but because he knows better.

God is good to all, but God loves, with a special, everlasting, covenantal love, those who are his people. They became his people by his doing, not their own, and he loved them before they were his people, even before he had created them. For his people, God is love to such a degree that he gave his Son to accomplish what they most needed: salvation from their sin and from his righteous wrath toward it. Toward these people, those whom God chose to be his own, he exercises his grace. "*Grace*," writes J. I. Packer, "is a New Testament technical term meaning love to the unlovely and seemingly unlovable, love that is primarily not a passion evoked by something in the loved one, but a purpose of making the loved great and glad: love that to this end gives, never mind the cost, and rescues those in need, never mind their unworthiness."[4]

Nothing will bring our Christian children greater peace in the hardest times they'll face than the assurance of love such as this from God. While they may not be able to see how a loving God could allow what is happening to them in a dark moment, they can remember the cross where God proved his love for his people. God became well acquainted with darkness and pain, precisely because he loves his people so much. Whatever the reason that God leads our Christian children through suffering, they can be sure it is *not* because he doesn't love them enough to intervene.

Things to Know

- God is good to all his creatures.
- Every good thing is a gift from God.
- God loves his people.
- God shows grace to his people, giving them what they do not deserve.
- God gave his own Son out of love for his people.

GOD IS INFINITE, IMMUTABLE, AND ETERNAL

Part of the humility we should train our children to feel toward God comes from the enormous distance between us as creatures and God as Creator. We are finite. We have limits. We can only be in one place at a time, only understand so much of a given situation, only stay awake so long. God is infinite. He has no limits. All that we have seen of what God is, he is without limit. Nothing restricts his power. No secret nugget of fact hides from his knowledge. He does not love, and love, and love—and then stop because he's reached his limit. While our children should know they can bring their fears, their doubts,

4. J. I. Packer, *Taking God Seriously: Vital Things We Need to Know* (Wheaton, IL: Crossway, 2013), 26.

and even their anger to God as to a caring Father, their stance should always be one of humility, the creature before the Creator, the finite before the Infinite. We cannot begin, with our limited, creaturely minds, to understand all the ways and intentions and plans of God. We sin if we assume we can.

All that God is, he has always been and always will be. God does not change; here our children will find a bedrock of assurance. God's love does not vary. His holiness does not budge. His power, his wisdom, and his grace toward them as his redeemed children cannot, and will not, ever change. There is richness in learning from the Bible who God is and what he is like. That richness grows only more precious when we add to it the knowledge that all God is, he will be without limit and forever.

Take older children outside on a starry night and ask them what they know about how big the universe is. How far away are the stars? How many stars are in the galaxy? How many galaxies are in the universe? Yet the Bible tells us that not even the heavens (big as they are) or the highest heavens can contain God (2 Chron. 6:18).

Like the Israelites in the wilderness clamoring for Aaron to make a golden calf, people of our day want a god with whom they can be comfortable. They want to imagine something a little more powerful than they are, as eager to serve them as they are to serve themselves, and call that "god." They want the god that feels right to them. Such a god is a make-believe god. It doesn't exist. God stands outside of us and all of his creation. We can know him only because he has graciously chosen to reveal himself to us, and we can know him only through his Word, the Bible.

The God of the Bible is the God described in the preceding pages. To learn about this God is to study what theologians call *theology proper*, that part of theology that is the actual study of what God himself is like. David Wells, after writing about the weighty glory of our holy God, asks, "Is this a matter so impractical that we can claim that it has nothing to do with our lives? Is this really so abstract that we can dismiss it as not being 'practical' and therefore irrelevant to what is important to us on a day-to-day basis?"[5] For children, too, knowing God, as he has revealed himself in Scripture, is fully relevant, fully practical, for all of life.

To live without knowing this God is to live without God. There is no other. On the other hand, to possess a sound knowledge of God's character is to be grounded on the surest foundation possible on which to build a human life. When our children know God's attributes, first in their minds as objective fact, then in their hearts as deeply felt assurance, they will be prepared for the worst—or for the best—that life can throw at them.

Things to Know

- God is infinite; nothing limits him.
- There is no limit to any of God's attributes.
- God is eternal, with no beginning and no end.
- Every one of God's attributes is eternal.
- Neither God nor his attributes ever change.

---

5. David Wells, *The Courage to Be Protestant: Truth-Lovers, Marketers, and Emergents in the Postmodern World* (Grand Rapids: Wm. B. Eerdmans Publishing Co., 2008), 133.

5

Scripture: What Is Truth?

"JUST BELIEVE"—WHAT?

In Western culture, the word "believe" has become freestanding, needing no object. "Just believe," we hear. Our culture doesn't care *what* we believe; it doesn't even matter if there is any *what* at all; it's enough to just believe. As far back as Disney's *Pinocchio*, a cheerful cricket sang that a child would get anything he desired if only his heart was in his dreams. Cinderella, too, assured children that if they just had faith in their dreams and kept on believing, their dreams and wishes would come true. Not only animated films, but many live-action, sports-themed movies also insist that the most unlikely championship will be won if only people *believe* it will happen.

One reason that our culture encourages belief while demonstrating indifference as to what is believed is that our world has shrunk. Transportation and communication advances have brought people of all kinds to live, think, and believe right next door to us. Every day, we rub shoulders with all kinds of different worldviews. Wanting to "be nice," we don't want to say a particular belief is wrong (i.e., untrue). Yet our children must learn the logic that A and non-A cannot be equally true at the same time.

I tell children that believing has no point unless the thing believed is worth believing. I might sincerely believe that I can fly. I might be 100 percent convinced of it. But my conviction doesn't make it true. If I climb to the top of the Empire State Building and throw myself off, flapping my arms, I will not survive the fall. Believing what is untrue not only accomplishes nothing, but it can also prove highly dangerous.

Faith in anything has only as much value as the object of that faith has reliability. To prepare them to live in our relativistic culture, we want to teach our children to ask, all the time, about whatever they see and hear, "Is it true?" And they need to know that truth exists, that it is independent of majority opinion, and that, at least to a degree, it can be known.

Another reason our culture so easily sets aside truth claims as matters of personal opinion is that, for some time now, our culture has magnified the "self," which fosters the idea that each separate self can access truth by looking within. The goals of *self*-esteem, *self*-fulfillment, *self*-gratification, *self*-expression have been taught, advertised, and exalted ad nauseam. This has proven fatal to faith in religious truth since so many have become so certain that God is, somehow, reached through the self. Even those who don't read the many books or attend the many classes on reaching God through the inner self feel that they "just know" what God is like. They rely on their own ideas, beliefs, and intuitions about God, never troubled by the least worry that their ideas could be wrong. Many in our culture who believe in God understand him and his character to be self-evident truth. They don't seem to care that what is evident about God to one person may be exactly the opposite of what is evident about God to someone else. This should rouse the desire to find a referee between competing ideas, an authoritative source that can clearly, objectively define *God*. For the most part, however, our contemporaries feel no such need. As long as each person is satisfied with his or her own idea of God, they think that all is well.

Children need to grow up with the understanding that, at its very core, Christianity consists of truth—objective, outside-of-me, whether-I-believe-it-or-not truth. While Christianity is more than *just* a set of correct beliefs, it certainly begins there. At its very heart, Christianity is *truth*, a series of propositional assertions and doctrinal statements. This truth—these truths—must be believed, or there is no Christianity.

Paul described the gospel as "the word of truth" (Eph. 1:13; Col. 1:5). He said that, when God grants repentance to people, it leads them "to a knowledge of the truth" (2 Tim. 2:25), and he said that people are saved through "belief in the truth" (2 Thess. 2:13). The word *doctrine* (meaning teaching) was not invented by people who want to sit at their desks and study theology. The apostles used this word and its synonyms in the New Testament (e.g., Rom. 16:17), and they received their mandate from Jesus himself. Of first importance to Jesus when he was on earth was his teaching ministry. Yes, he worked miracles, both to establish his identity as the Messiah and to demonstrate compassion. But when the disciples came looking for him to bring him back to the waiting, needy crowds, he said he had to go on to other cities to preach there, because that was why he had come (Mark 1:37–38). As David Wells points out, this teaching of Jesus is what the apostles explained and expanded, writing it down in their epistles. "To be a believer," Wells writes, "is to believe this teaching." Then he continues, "Christians, therefore, are those who 'know' this doctrine. They 'believe' it, 'have' it, 'hold it fast,' 'guard' it, and 'contend earnestly' for it. . . . They . . . treasure it, teach it, defend it, and are nourished in their lives by its truths."[1] This is what Christianity *is*, and this is what home and church must be teaching children.

Things to Know

- There are things that are true, always and everywhere.
- Truth does not change.
- Truth is true for everyone—even for those who do not believe it.
- Believing only has value when the thing believed is true.
- Believing what is not true is dangerous.
- Christianity is made up of truths to be believed.
- Christians are required to know, believe, teach, and defend the truth.

WE NEED A REVELATION

Early on, children must learn that we cannot know God apart from his own revelation of himself. The distance between an infinite, holy God and a finite, sinful human is far greater than the distance between your child's goldfish and your child. Little Goldie can never

---

1. David Wells, *The Courage to Be Protestant: Truth-Lovers, Marketers, and Emergents in the Postmodern World* (Grand Rapids: Wm. B. Eerdmans Publishing Co., 2008), 228–29.

comprehend how and why your child does what he does, nor does your child have any means of communicating that information to his fish. God, on the other hand, though he is so very different from us, created us with the capacity to understand something of the revelation he graciously provides. While we can learn from God's revelation, it is absurd to suppose that we can understand him without it.

You can teach the idea of revelation to your children by telling them you're thinking of a word and then asking them to tell you what that word is. They can guess and guess and guess, but will (probably) never guess the word. They need a revelation. Or write a short story telling two or three details from your childhood. Put the story in a sealed envelope. Give the envelope to a child, but don't allow her to open it. Challenge her and any other children present to tell you the story. They can't; they need a revelation. When something is hidden and cannot be seen or understood, a revelation is needed to make it known. Have your children imagine a great artist who has worked in secret on a masterpiece and has allowed no one to see it. When he finally invites his friends to gather around the canvas and then pulls off the covering drape so that, now, all can see it, he has revealed what they could never have imagined otherwise.

God wants his people to know him, so he has graciously revealed himself to us. He has revealed himself in two kinds of revelation: general revelation and special revelation. General revelation can be seen and heard by anyone. Paul discusses it in Romans 1, when he speaks of creation and how all men know, from it, that God exists and that he possesses great power. In Romans 2, Paul points out another form of general revelation, and that is the conscience. All humans have an innate sense of right and wrong which God himself has placed there in order to reveal something of his character and his requirements.

General revelation leaves human beings without an excuse for their failure to worship and serve God. No one can say, "I had no idea there was such a thing as God!" Yet, while several of God's attributes may be guessed at when we look at creation, they are really only guesses until we read what he has revealed of himself in his Word. This is special revelation—God communicating specifics about what he is like to humans so they may have a relationship with him. General revelation, creation, and conscience can never show us God's plan of salvation. For that, we must have the Bible.

In our shrinking world, our children will have many friends, neighbors, and colleagues who are certain that their own idea of God is correct. They will insist that our children's ideas of God are either wrong or at least no truer than their own, very different ideas. Sure, Christianity has wise, religious teachings in the Bible, our children will hear, but other religions have books that are just as good. An understanding of the Bible as the Word of God, unknowable until God revealed it, will fortify our children to stand alone against the majority consensus that all ideas about God are equally valid.

Things to Know

- We need a revelation from God to know the truth about him.
- A revelation is truth that is made known to us that we would never have known on our own.
- God has revealed himself to us so his people will know him.
- God has given all men general revelation, things anyone can see that show us there is a God.
- God has given special revelation in the Bible, the only source for knowing what God is like and how to have a right relationship with him.

ONE-OF-A-KIND

Children need to know that the Bible is truly unique. It is a one-of-a-kind book, and there is no other like it. The Bible is one large book in which are gathered many smaller books. These books were written over hundreds of years by at least forty-four different authors. Yet God is the author of it all. No other book is like that. God did not "take over" those human authors so that they acted as robots, doing what he made them do. The human authors had ideas and chose words and wrote down what we read in our Bibles. Yet the Bible claims that it is the Word of God. In some instances, God actually told the human authors what he wanted written, so that they quoted him. We find this when one of the prophets says, "Thus says the Lord." In other cases, God worked through the circumstances and the personalities of the human authors so that, while they wrote what they wanted to say, they were also writing the very Word of God. No other book has God as its ultimate author. This is what Paul means when he writes, "All Scripture is breathed out by God and profitable for teaching, for reproof, for correction, and for training in righteousness" (2 Tim. 3:16). Peter speaks of this too: "For no prophecy was ever produced by the will of man, but men spoke from God as they were carried along by the Holy Spirit" (2 Peter 1:21).

Things to Know

- The Bible is a unique book.
- The Bible had many different human authors.
- The Bible's ultimate author is God.
- Human authors wrote what they meant to write, yet God directed what they wrote.
- This is what we mean by "inspired by God" or "breathed out by God."
- The Bible alone is the Word of God.

WHY DO WE CALL IT *SCRIPTURE*?

Give your children a fairly long sentence to remember, word for word. Tell them you will ask them later to repeat it to you. Be sure several interesting things happen between telling them this sentence and asking them to repeat it to you. Chances are, they will not be able to reproduce it exactly as you said it. Ask them what would happen if you had something really long to say, something that might take half an hour to explain, and you wanted them to remember it exactly several days from now. What could they do? They may say they could write it down as you said it. This is what God did when he revealed himself to us. He gave us his special revelation in written form, so we could remember it forever. God had people write it down so we could copy and recopy his revelation, passing it down year after year and century after century. The word *scripture* comes from the Latin word *scriptare*, to write. The holy scriptures are God's Word written down so we can keep it forever.

God gave a rich gift by giving us his Word, and he made it even richer by giving us that Word written down. Anyone who can read—or who can listen to reading—can know what God is like. No greater comfort will our children find when they face suffering and trials than the confidence that they know their God and that he remains the same, even when life's circumstances change for the worse. They can rest certain that it is the true God they know because they know him from his revealed Word. They can be sure their most dreadful dark times will end in a burst of everlasting light because they have promises, passed on and written down, from God himself. They don't have to just "hope so"; they don't have to just whistle in the dark; they can *know* because they know that what the Bible says, God has said.

Derek Thomas, in his commentary on the book of Job, comments on Job's remark in the midst of his suffering. Job, having lost everything, said:

> But he knows the way that I take;
>   when he has tried me, I shall come out as gold.
> My foot has held fast to his steps;
>   I have kept his way and have not turned aside.
> I have not departed from the commandment of his lips;
>   I have treasured the words of his mouth more than my portion of
>   food. (Job 23:10–12)

Thomas writes that wise advice to suffering Christians is "to learn what God's Word has to say, and to discover how relevant it all is. Disciplined, thoughtful Bible study will pay enormous dividends. It will change the way we think, and that in turn will change the way we live *and feel.*" More than that, Thomas continues, "We should *seek to know God's Word in advance.* 'I have hidden your word in my heart that I might not sin against you' (Ps. 119:11). When trouble comes, it is too late to start learning what God has to say. Like some of God's creatures, we must learn to hide stores of food for long, cold winter months."[2]

Sinclair Ferguson makes the same comparison of storing up supplies of God's truth for trials sure to come some day. "Learn the promises of God in advance," he writes. "When the time of crisis or darkness comes, it is too late." He urges Christians to store up those promises, like a squirrel stores up nuts for winter; the time will come "when you will need God's promises to act as an anchor for your soul."[3] As an example, Ferguson cites the time in his own life when his brother had just died and it was going to fall to him to report this sad circumstance to their mother. Difficult as it was to lose a brother, to have to break the news to his mom made it far worse, and Ferguson was troubled thinking about it. Then, however, he remembered Romans 8 with its many promises of comfort for hard times. Those words, he writes, "lodged for many years in my memory, seemed to grow from a seed into a mighty tree under whose branches I found shelter from the storm, comfort in my sorrow, and light in my darkness."[4]

Things to Know

- *Scriptures* means "writings."
- God ordained that his Word be written down so we could keep it and know it through the centuries.
- God's Word provides guidance and encouragement for all of life.
- When Christians study God's Word regularly, they will have what they need for life as they need it.

REQUIRED TO KNOW

Just as "I didn't know" is no excuse for breaking the law of the land, so it is no excuse for failing to worship and serve the true God.

---

2. Derek Thomas, *The Storm Breaks: Job Simply Explained* (Webster, NY: Evangelical Press, 2005), 193–94.

3. Sinclair B. Ferguson, *Deserted By God?* (Carlisle, PA: Banner of Truth Trust, 2013), 14.

4. Ibid., 27.

God has made himself known. He has given us a whole book in which he shows us what he is like. We are his creatures and he created us with this primary purpose in mind: "to glorify God and to enjoy him forever."[5] We can't know him well enough to glorify him and neither can we enjoy him if we don't know what he's like. We are required to know. "What does the Bible primarily teach?" asks the Westminster Shorter Catechism. The answer: "What man *must* believe about God and what God *requires* of man" (italics added).[6]

Nor is it enough to know bits and pieces of God's Word. Error comes in when only parts of the truth are studied or only some truths are cherished. In the Bible, God has given us the story of the redemption he accomplished for us. The story begins when he created the first human beings and moves through man's deliberate fall into sin. The story continues down the rocky road of sinful man's endlessly failing attempts to reconcile himself to God, even as God continues to work, through grace, to reconcile man without man's help. The story covers the first whispered promises of grace, God's initial covenant with his people, pictures of redemption, laws revealing the holy character of God, a sacrificial system picturing what man needed, and threats and promises thundered by the prophets. Besides all this, the Bible also contains songs to use in worship, directions for wise living in all areas of life, stories of the Messiah and his teaching, complex explanations of doctrine, practical points on living the Christian life, and glances ahead at Messiah's return—and all of it is intended to reveal our God to us. We must take the time to hear, read, study, and learn what is in the Word of God.

The good news is that, though the Bible's authorship makes it unique, in other ways it is a book like any book. Ordinary, normal people who know how to read—or at least who can listen to reading—can understand the Bible. It is not written in secret code. Except for a few, clearly symbolic passages, it is not loaded with symbols. It does not hide

5. Douglas Kelly and Philip Rollinson, *The Westminster Shorter Catechism in Modern English* (Phillipsburg, NJ: Presbyterian and Reformed Publishing Company, 1986), 5.
6. Ibid.

layers of allegories that only the specially trained can understand. It is a book, and it is to be read like other books. The reader assumes the words on the page have the ordinary meaning those words usually have. The reader applies the same rules for reading and comprehending any book to reading and comprehending the Bible. While there are parts of the Bible that would be less interesting for children to read and other parts that would surely raise questions, much of the Bible can be read by any child who can read—and it can be understood by that child as well. God gave it to reveal truth, not to hide it. The Bible is clear and easy to understand.

That does not mean that it's always easy to accept or easy to obey. In the sense of spiritually understanding the Bible, sinners are at a great disadvantage. Their minds and their wills are so steeped in sin that, even when the clear, simple sense of the words of Scripture are before them, they may not "get it." God's Word has such power that it can give a sinner life or change a believer's attitudes and practice, but only when God the Holy Spirit gives spiritual understanding. The theological term for this is "illumination." You can illustrate it to your children with a window-less room. Place a treat of some kind in the room, then lead your child into the room in the dark—without turning on the light—and invite her to help herself to the treat. The treat is there, but your child cannot see it. Turn on the light. Once the room—and your child's eyes—have been illuminated, once the light has come on, what was there all along becomes plain. So the Holy Spirit causes us to "see," with spiritually opened eyes, truth that was there all along. This is why we teach our children to pray before they read God's Word, asking God to make clear to them what he wants them to know from it.

Things to Know

- We are required to know God's Word.
- God's Word contains one big story: God's saving his people from sin.
- God's Word contains moral laws, rules for worship, wise directions, doctrine, and promises.

- The intent of all of Scripture is to reveal God.
- We must become familiar with all of God's Word.
- The same rules for reading and understanding other books work for the Bible.
- The Bible is clear and easy to understand.
- We need the Holy Spirit's illumination to enable us to spiritually understand the Bible.
- Illumination causes us to see, spiritually speaking, the truth of God's Word.

IN WHOSE OPINION?

In the wisdom of our culture, so much confidence rests in each individual self that, for most people, whatever the self feels to be true of God or of any moral or practical matter certainly must be true. It is each individual self that sits in judgment upon any scriptures, deciding which, if any, religion's scriptures it accepts and then deciding which specific passages in those scriptures it believes and which it doesn't. The only place this does not hold true is in matters of political correctness. Once our culture declares a particular opinion politically incorrect or intolerant, no one can hold that opinion with any degree of credibility. As more and more of what the Bible calls morally wrong becomes embraced by our culture as right and admirable, it becomes harder to proclaim the truths of God's Word upon moral matters. When Christians call certain behaviors "wrong," they find themselves vilified as hateful and unenlightened. Yet Christians must continue to count as wrong what Scripture clearly teaches as morally wrong. Knowing that it is God himself—the one from whom all moral law derives—who has said certain practices are sinful will help our children to resist waves of human opinion, however popular. A clear awareness of God's moral law can drown out the name-calling our children will face when they call evil *evil*, no matter what others call it.

Even among professing Christians, common practice upon encountering a biblical teaching that "doesn't sound right" is to explain it away or simply ignore it. Yet, if, as the Bible claims about itself and as

Christianity claims for it, the Bible is the very Word of God, then, of necessity, the Bible possesses all authority regarding all it claims to be true. The Bible is not just preferred teachings for Christians. The Bible is what God said, put into writing. He whose creatures we are and who, therefore, defines all things and makes all rules, has spoken. Our only legitimate response is to hear, accept, believe, and obey. Whenever we understand truth one way, then learn that the Bible teaches something different, it is our understanding we must correct, and the Bible's assertion we must embrace. Our children must grow up seeing us set aside our own opinions whenever those opinions bump up against the Bible's teaching in disagreement. As Eli said, when he learned God's hard word regarding him and his sons, "It is the Lord; let him do what seems good to him" (1 Sam. 3:18). When we truly understand what the Bible is, our own ideas, opinions, and values must always bow before its teaching. When we understand, concerning any matter, that "thus says the Lord," there is nothing else for us to say, nothing else for us to believe. God's Word is supreme.

Things to Know

- God's people must consider wrong whatever the Bible says is wrong.
- The Bible is the final word because it is God's Word.
- Christians must intentionally bring their minds under the authority of God's Word.

6

Humanity: "What a Piece of Work Is a Man!"[1]

Death narrates the tale told in *The Book Thief.* The story takes place during the difficult years of World War II. It focuses on simple, ordinary people in a small town in Germany, people who are not at all convinced that Hitler's policies are best for Germans, let alone for the rest of the world. In *The Book Thief,* Death introduces us to people whose lives fill with suffering because of Hitler and the inhumane things he and his Nazis inflict upon others. Death also shows us everyday citizens who choose to risk their own safety to reach out to alleviate, in whatever small ways they can, the suffering of others. Death ends his narration with these words:

> I am constantly overestimating and underestimating the human race . . . I wanted to ask her how the same thing could be so ugly and so glorious, and its words and stories so damning and brilliant. . . .
> * * * A LAST NOTE FROM YOUR NARRATOR * * *
> I am haunted by humans.[2]

Blaise Pascal wrote of the same paradox. He said that any true religion would have to describe man as both great and glorious, more so than any other creature, and still horribly wretched and evil. The religion must then, he added, "account for such amazing contradictions."[3] Pascal went

---

1. William Shakespeare, *Hamlet*, in *The Complete Works of Shakespeare*, 3rd ed., ed. David Bevington (Glenview, IL: Scott, Foresman, and Company, 1980), 2.2.304–305.
2. Markus Zusak, *The Book Thief* (New York: Alfred A. Knopf, 2007), 550.
3. "Man's greatness and wretchedness are so evident that the true religion must necessarily teach us that there is in man some great principle of greatness and some great principle of

on to say that Christianity provides an explanation for both the greatness of man and his desperate depravity. Only Christianity views man as exalted—"a little lower than the heavenly beings and crowned . . . with glory and honor" (Ps. 8:5)—and ruined in every part—"They have all turned aside; together they have become corrupt; there is none who does good, not even one" (Ps. 14:3). We see examples of both every day. Man achieves astounding accomplishments, through his intellect, through his art, and through his goodness and compassion. Who hasn't had the experience of being in a difficult spot and having a complete stranger offer help? Yet each day's headlines carry fresh instances of humans inflicting horror and suffering on other humans—not, like animals, to protect themselves or in order to survive, but just because they can.

The culture in which we are raising our children and the culture in which they will live as adults is so confused on the answer to the psalmist's question "What is man?" that it seems to speak out of both sides of its mouth. On the one hand, our culture so exalts other creatures that it raises them to the same level as humans, consequently bringing humans down to the level of any other created being. Often, the people forming political lobbies and demanding measures to save certain endangered species of birds, animals, and even insects are the same people demanding the right to kill unborn humans. "What gives humans the right to use animals?" they would ask. "How dare humans consider themselves superior to other species? Humans may be a little further evolved, but nothing more." Nor is this something only seen in political lobbies. On a popular level, many people are as emotionally connected to their pets as they would be to children.

On the other hand, our culture so exalts human beings as to put them on a level with God. Once God was considered the ultimate authority to whom every human would ultimately answer. Now, however, the highest good is to fulfill myself, to follow my own ideas of right and wrong; self-denial for God's sake is out, and my own happiness, not God's will, is very much in. Nor is this just the attitude of a few rebels

wretchedness. It must also account for such amazing contradictions." Blaise Pascal, *Pensees* (London: Penguin Books, 1995), 46.

on the fringes of society; this is the normative way of thinking. To put anything before the happiness of the self is seen as pathological.

Our children need to understand what Christianity teaches about human beings, because they themselves are human beings and because, without a biblical concept of who man is and what he needs, they can never understand the salvation God provides or explain that salvation to anyone else.

CREATED

Human beings are created beings. They share this characteristic with everything else that exists, except God. God alone is the uncreated Creator. While humans have much that elevates them above all other creatures, still, they take their place with every other created being underneath the supreme rule of the God who made them. As wonderful as humans are, they are closer to a single-celled amoeba in their creatureliness and finitude than they are to the infinite, uncreated God. Many of our contemporaries think highly enough of themselves to assume that they have complete access to the divine whenever they want it, and that on their own terms. They fail to realize that, even apart from the question of man's sin and God's holiness, there still exists a tremendous distance between man and God, a distance that modern people seldom notice. They fail to think how dependent they are on someone outside themselves. They lack any sense of reverence or submission before the One to whom they owe their existence, and they never consider that they exist to please him, not themselves.

We can lead our children in considering what it means to be a creature by encouraging them to consider their own creations. When they make a drawing or a sandwich or an airplane model did they have a purpose in mind for it? Once they've made it, whose is it? Who gets to decide what to do with it? This illustrates one aspect of our relationship as creatures with God. To be created is to belong to the Creator. As the psalmist wrote, "It is he who made us, and we are his" (Ps. 100:3). A creator has a purpose for making his creations. The creations themselves do not get to decide whether or not they will fit in with the creator's purposes. Your child's sandwich does not get to choose whether or not there will be mayonnaise on it. It does not choose whether it will be consumed right now or packed in a lunch for tomorrow. The sandwich's creator decides. While God did make humans with the ability to make choices, ultimately, all God's creatures fulfill his purposes for them. Seeking to live apart from him and his will is as ridiculous as your child's sandwich deciding to be a sock instead of a sandwich. If our children master this idea of God as Creator with absolute rights over them, it will make one more line of defense for them against bitterness or despair when circumstances arise that they would not have chosen. Or when, as adults, they watch others receive the success or the acclaim, the families or the careers that they wanted, but did not get, it will bring peace to remember that they are God's and that he disposes of them according to his wise purposes.

Things to Know

- Man is a creature.
- God, as Creator, is infinitely greater than man, the creature.
- Man belongs to God his Creator.

"IN THE IMAGE OF GOD HE CREATED HIM"[4]

While our children should learn humility as creatures before their Creator, they should also take their rightful place of honor over all other creatures because God chose to make only humans in his own image. Consider, with your children, how humans are like God in ways that none of the animals, birds, or fish are. Consider the human ability to think and to create. Have your child choose a living creature and list the things that creature can make. Birds can make nests, beavers can make dams, rabbits can make warrens. The creatures' abilities to make these things show us the wisdom of God in how he designed them. A bird, however, can only build its basic nest, the same in design as every other bird of its species. What bird ever built his house with a porch? Or sculpted statues to stand inside the entry? What beaver ever planned and made an attractive bridge

---

4. Gen. 1:27.

across his dam? What rabbit community ever engineered something like a skyscraper with multiple dwellings for their warren? Only humans can imagine, think, plan, and execute these things.

When humans exercise the creativity God gave them, they find all kinds of uses for his other creatures. To man alone, God gave dominion over the rest of creation. Have your children list some created items that birds and animals use. Birds find uses for twigs, sticks, and soft materials for their nests. They use seeds, bugs, or worms for their meals. Bears and foxes use holes in the rock or in the ground for a dry home. An otter uses the water both for his grocery store and for his recreational park. Again, we see God's wisdom in how he gave the animals instincts that cause them to find and use what they need to survive. But could a fox consider a cocoa bean and figure out how to use it to make hot chocolate? Could a bear realize rock walls could be made exactly to order if he mixed sand, rock, and water and made concrete? Could an otter use wood, steel, and electricity to build a roller coaster? God rules supremely over all he has made, but he shared that dominion with man when he put him over the rest of creation and told him to subdue it and to exercise dominion over every living thing (Gen. 1:28).

Ask your child to name ways that creatures communicate with each other. If you have a pet, consider specifically ways it communicates with you. A horse pins back its ears when it's angry and thrusts its head and its ears forward when it's curious or eager. What does your dog mean when it growls or when it whines or when it barks? Horses call to other horses in the distance, and dogs mark their territory to let other dogs know this is theirs. But can a horse tell another horse what it did yesterday? Can it tell that horse what it hopes to do tomorrow? (For that matter, can a horse even make plans or have hopes, besides the plan to hurry home after a ride and the hope of finding some good hay to munch on when it gets there?) Can a dog explain to another dog how he met his master or what he likes best about going on walks with that master? God wanted people with whom he could have a relationship, so he made them in his own image. He made them able to communicate with each other and with him.

When a wolf pack isolates a baby reindeer from its herd, attacks it, and eats it, are the wolves being bad? When animals kill each other, are they wicked? When a duck moves in and snatches a piece of food from the bill of another duck, is it stealing? Is this duck an evil duck? Your child (if he's old enough) will recognize that this is just how animals behave. It's part of how they survive in the wild. These things aren't wrong for them. In fact, as far as animals are concerned, there's no such thing as right and wrong. They are not equipped to know the difference. They have no conscience. Man, however, is like God in that he is a moral creature. He knows what's right and what's wrong, even when he's never had a chance to sit down and study the Word of God (which is our ultimate, objective source of right and wrong). God has put a conscience within every human and though, because of sin, it has become distorted, it still exists. When humans rob from, hurt, or kill other humans, they *are* bad or wicked or evil. They are guilty before God for immoral behavior.

Most importantly, humans can enter into covenants with other people and with God, and they can worship. Your child's dog loves him. It gets very excited when your child comes home, jumping all over him and licking him. But the dog can know nothing about its Creator. The dog has no concept of prayer or praise. While the dog glorifies God by being a dog as God created it to be, the dog does this unconsciously and in ignorance. It cannot know God. Humans were made in the image of God so that they could deliberately, consciously understand something of the wonder of who God is and love and worship him for it. God honored humans supremely by choosing them alone with whom to make a covenant. As far as we know from Scripture, not even the angels are in a covenant relationship with God. "What is man," cried David in wonder, "that you are mindful of him, and the son of man that you care for him?" (Ps. 8:4).

Things to Know

- God created man, and no other creature, in the image of God.
- This places man over all the other creatures.

- Humans can think and create.
- God gave man dominion over all the earth.
- Humans can communicate.
- Humans know right from wrong.
- Humans can enter into covenants with each other and with God.

"MALE AND FEMALE HE CREATED THEM"[5]

It would seem that something as basic as maleness and female-ness in human beings would pose no complicated problems for the understanding. Yet, throughout human history (at least, throughout fallen human history), humans have had trouble getting this right. For millennia, sinful male humans, being physically stronger, have not only oppressed individual female humans, but made it a matter of policy that women were inferior in every way, not to be trusted, not to be considered, given no rights, and allowed no influence in decisions. Even in these modern times, many countries in the world make such oppression of women national policy. In such countries, simply being born female guarantees a lifestyle similar to that of a prisoner. The education of girls in these countries may be neglected; women are not allowed the freedom to come and go as they please; they may not have drivers' licenses; they may not hold office or, in some cases, even vote; they must be covered from head to toe if there is any chance they may be seen; they are given in marriage to men whom they do not love or even know, according to the desires of their fathers or brothers.

In understandable reaction to this injustice, female humans in Western countries have created movements to demand changes in such thinking and to insist upon rights for women. However, as is so often the case where injustice has been so engrained, the pendulum has swung to the other extreme, and women insist they are exactly like men in every way so that there should be no differences whatever between men and women and what they do. Yet, the very makeup of male and female bodies, both in terms of size and strength and in

5. Gen. 1:27.

terms of reproductive capabilities, should make it clear to anyone that men and women are *not* identical. Nor, in some important ways, are they interchangeable.

In the first pages of the Bible, we have the account of God making the first man and then saying it was not good for him to be alone. What God, in his wisdom and goodness, then created was not more male humans, exactly like the first, but a female human, similar in many ways, yet different, too. Christians must walk the biblical tightrope between making too much of men at the expense of women and making too much of women at the expense of men.

We must raise our sons as men, strong enough to protect a wife and do all that's needed to realize her greatest potential (Eph. 5:25–28), but gentle enough to invest time in understanding the things that matter to a wife (1 Peter 3:7). We must raise our daughters to appreciate their unique calling as women, capable of wonderful things men cannot do, as well as capable of many things men can do, training them to understand that there is no dishonor in choosing to submit to a husband as God commands, since God the Son himself submits to God the Father (Eph. 5:22–24; 1 Peter 3:5; Matt. 26:39; 1 Cor. 11:3; 15:28).

Nor is our culture confused only about specific roles of men and women, husbands and wives. Increasingly, other options—bisexuality, transsexuality, homosexuality—rate high in popular opinion. Though it will result in painful misunderstanding in which people, intending no harm to anyone, are labeled hate-filled or homophobes, our children must learn that Christians stand firm on God's Word, even when most others rage against it. As J. I. Packer points out, it is the sovereign God who made us who "states ideals for, and sets limits to, human behavior. . . . One restrictive maxim spelled out in both Testaments is that the only right place for gratifying our sexual drive, huge and hungry as it may be, is within monogamous marriage, where mutual sexual pleasure is designed to further both pair bonding and procreation. Homosexual acts are explicitly ruled out. . . . Let it be said that all Christians have lifelong battles with similarly unruly desires in some form, although few such desires are hailed as good and glamorized in the way that homosexual urgings are in today's Western societies."[6]

Things to Know

- God created human beings male and female.
- God chooses which gender each human baby will be.
- Men and women need each other.
- While men and women are equals in many ways, including their value as persons, they also have important differences.
- Sexuality is a good gift, to be used only in a one-man, one-woman marriage.

SINFUL IN EVERY PART

Pascal was right. And to quote Shakespeare, man is not only "noble in reason . . . express and admirable . . . like an angel . . . like a god . . . the beauty of the world,"[7] he is also thoroughly wretched. Humans are "plunged into the wretchedness of their blindness and concupiscence, which has become their second nature."[8] Man, created to exercise dominion over the rest of creation, finds that "all creatures either distress or tempt him, and dominate him."[9] Any worldview, to possess credibility, must explain how something as wonderful as man became so wretched.

The Bible teaches that man was made in the image of his Creator, wonderful in the unique nature God had given. The Bible also teaches that the first man, by his own choice, gave in to sin which then became his second nature, passed on to every human ever conceived. We teach our children that people don't become sinners by sinning; they sin because they are sinners.

We can illustrate for children the idea of a sinful nature by explaining to them that the nature of something determines what it is and what

6. J. I. Packer, *Taking God Seriously: Vital Things We Need to Know* (Wheaton, IL: Crossway, 2013), 29.
7. Shakespeare, *Hamlet*, 2.2.305–308.
8. Pascal, *Pensees*, 48.
9. Pascal, *Pensees*, 47.

it is not. It is the nature of a rock to not move. It is the nature of water to be wet. Birds fly because they are birds. It's in their nature to fly. A coyote howls at the moon because that's what coyotes do; it's in their nature. People don't sin once, then sin again and, little by little, become sinners. They sin because they are sinners. Fish swim because they are fish; they cannot *not* swim. So sinners cannot *not* sin.

A dog has a doggy nature; it barks, wags its tail, and sniffs everything because it is a dog. That's what dogs do. Spot may usually live in the backyard. One day, his master takes him to the woods and removes his collar. He's free! He's free to chase squirrels, he's free to dig holes, but Spot is *not* free to fly. Spot is only free to do the things that his doggy nature allows him to do. But he doesn't mind; Spot doesn't want to fly. It's not in his nature to want to fly.

People are not forced to sin, in the sense of someone making them sin against their will. People are free to not sin, but only in the same way that a dog is free to not fly. Sinners are free to live perfectly righteous lives all the time; no one is stopping them, but they cannot. They do not even want to. Consistently righteous living is simply not in a sinner's nature.

Humans remain wonderful, the only creatures made in the image of God. But humans are born in sin and every part of them—body, mind, emotions, and will—are affected by sin. This is not to say that every human is bad as he could be. We rejoice in the restraining grace of God, who does not allow human sin to run rampant but holds sinners back. Yet every human ever born (except the Lord Jesus) is affected in every part by his sinfulness.

Sin has become an old-fashioned word, sneered at by our contemporaries. Sin implies an objective standard of right and wrong, which necessitates an authority outside of ourselves to declare what that standard is. The Bible, seeing God as that authority, has no qualms about speaking, often and strongly, about sin. People of our time deny that objective standards exist at all, so how can there be right and wrong? Virtue, both as a word and as a concept, has been replaced with values. Virtue required a standard; values have their source in each individual's preferences.

Similarly, as David Wells points out, sin and true, legitimate guilt have had to step aside and make way for shame. Shame is an emotion and may have nothing to do with reality, only with perception. I feel shame over a blemish on my skin (though I did not cause it), over the part of town where I live (though I had nothing to do with its decline), over my tendency to look at things on the Internet I shouldn't view. Shame is an emotion that slows down my personal development, a disease that must be cured. It doesn't involve guilt that must be pardoned. Our children grow up in a culture that assumes people are basically good and innocent. It believes therapists must help us with our shame, but sees no need of a God to pardon our guilt.[10]

Consequently, language of sin and guilt, of reconciliation and forgiveness, is foreign to those who surround us, but it must not be foreign to our children. Children need to grow up understanding that, when they disobey their parents, they don't just disappoint their parents; they displease a holy God. At the same time, they need to know that they disobey their parents because they are sinners, just as their parents disobey the God they love because they themselves are sinners. As children and as adults, they need a biblical understanding of man, in his sublimity and in his depravity. If they love God, they will be deeply disappointed in themselves when they sin, especially when the sin is in an area where they have failed repeatedly. At the same time, if they have a biblical understanding of themselves as sinful human beings, they will not despair. They will understand that this is how it is on this side of heaven. When others sin against them or against those they love, in horrific, deplorable ways, they will have, not cynicism, but a certain "What-else-should-we-expect?" attitude to sustain them. They will understand that people are sinners and sin because of it.

With a biblical understanding of man, our children can value human beings supremely and live out that understanding in a lifetime of ministry and service. They can remain standing through a lifetime's onslaught of sin, their own and that of others. And they will realize

10. David Wells, *The Courage to Be Protestant: Truth-Lovers, Marketers, and Emergents in the Postmodern World* (Grand Rapids: Wm. B. Eerdmans Publishing Co., 2008), 162–63.

why the gospel, with its message of forgiveness and reconciliation, alone provides the solution to the wretchedness of man that Pascal highlighted in his paradox.

Things to Know

- God created man righteous.
- The first human beings rebelled against God, bringing sin into the world.
- Every human since has been born a sinner.
- We all have a sinful nature; it is in our nature to sin.
- Left to ourselves, sinners are unable to *not* sin.
- Sin affects every part of every human being.
- Even Christians will not be free of all sin until they reach heaven.

7

Jesus Christ: "But Who Do You Say That I Am?"[1]

The question was all-important when Jesus asked it of his disciples and has continued all-important to this day. Jesus had first asked what people in general thought of him. Other people had all sorts of ideas about who Jesus was: John the Baptist or Elijah or Jeremiah or another of the prophets. What mattered for the disciples, though, was not what others thought. "But who do *you* say that I am?" Jesus wanted to know.

In our day, people hold far more ideas of who Jesus is than they did when Jesus first asked, and those ideas possess much greater variety than they did back then. Ask Jesus' question of fifty different people on a busy city street, and you will no doubt receive fifty different answers. As Jesus assured Simon Peter, who answered for the disciples when Jesus first asked, there *is* a right answer. Peter responded, "You are the Christ, the Son of the living God," and this answer provides the concise form of the Christian church's teaching about Jesus through the ages. It is an answer that can be unpacked in great detail, and the riches of that unpacking are what we want our children to learn about Jesus as they grow. It is what they will need in order to repent and believe in the first place, since Christianity is, first of all, faith in the Lord Jesus Christ as he is revealed in Scripture. It is what they will need to grow in the faith once they've begun. Writing for *Modern Reformation*, Graeme Goldsworthy says, "Every Christian needs to grow in grace and in the knowledge of our Lord Jesus Christ (2 Peter 3:18). The knowledge of Christ includes

1. Matt. 16:15.

understanding his person and work in all their multifaceted characteristics. . . . While 'Jesus died for my sins' is one expression of saving faith, no Christian can grow toward maturity on such a basic diet."[2]

WHO HE IS

Very few people would deny that Jesus of Nazareth lived and died. The question is, who was he? A revolutionary? An itinerant moral teacher who ran afoul of the authorities? A victim of circumstances? The Christian answer has always been Peter's: "You are the Christ, the Son of the living God" (Matt. 16:16). Many want to deny that Jesus was divine. They claim that the apostles came along later, after Jesus had died, and wrote epistles that claimed he was divine. You can take your children on a treasure hunt through the Gospels to look for places where Jesus made claims about himself that could only be true if he really was God. (The best gospel account for finding these is John's.) You can take them on another treasure hunt looking for things Jesus did in the gospel narratives that he could only have done if he was divine.

The Bible's teaching is that Jesus Christ is the divine Son of God, who never had a beginning but who always existed. Everything that the Father can do, Jesus can do. All the authority and all the glory that the Father has, the Son has too. In the almost unbelievable grace of the Trinity, God the Father planned a salvation for his ruined people that involved sending his Son to become one of them, and his Son willingly agreed.

Jesus' life did not begin when he was born in Bethlehem, and neither did it begin when he was conceived by the power of the Holy Spirit in Mary. Jesus had always existed as God. What began when Gabriel told Mary she would conceive was Jesus' human life. He took on not just a human body, but a complete human nature, body and soul. You can ask your children what a puppy would be if its mother was a purebred collie and its father was a purebred German shepherd. They will probably tell you the puppy would be half collie, half German shepherd, and they

2. Graeme Goldsworthy, "Faith in the Real Jesus: Understanding Him as Prophet, Priest, and King," *Modern Reformation*, November/December 2013, 36.

would be right. But when we consider that Jesus' mother was a human being and Jesus' Father was God, we don't end up with someone who was half man, half God. Jesus is 100 percent human and 100 percent God. Not only that, but Jesus will remain 100 percent human and 100 percent divine forever. Having taken on a human nature and become like us, he will always keep that human nature, and it is a real human body we will see when we see Jesus in heaven.

Jesus is unique in the universe. He is one person who possesses two natures. No being anywhere has two natures. There is no such thing as an animal that is 100 percent dog and 100 percent cat. Your child is one person with one nature. Even God the Father has only one nature—a divine nature. The Son of God alone has two complete and perfect natures, one human, one divine, united in one person. There is a mystery to this, as there is with a number of things having to do with God. How could one person grow in knowledge and learn things, like any human, *and* simultaneously be the all-seeing, all-knowing God? How could one person live in a body, limited in space and time like any human, *and* be the omnipresent God? Christian doctrine affirms both of Jesus, perfect humanity and perfect deity. Another profitable treasure hunt in one of the Gospels could involve making two lists as you read with your children, one of times when Jesus' actions resembled that of any other human and one of times when Jesus' actions were clearly those of God.

The first miracle involving Jesus, and the one from which all the others spring, is the miracle of the incarnation. The angel promised Mary she would have a Son, but Mary worried that she had not been with a man. A baby can't have a mother only; a baby requires a father as well. The first great miracle in the Gospels was that Mary became pregnant with Jesus, and there was no human father. Gabriel provided an explanation, but it was an explanation that still retains the mystery: the Holy Spirit would come upon Mary, and the power of the Most High would overshadow her. "Therefore," the angel told her, "the child to be born will be called holy—the Son of God" (Luke. 1:35). It is because this child who grew to be a man was also God that he was able to do all the miracles of which we read in the Gospels, and it is also why he could do what was necessary to save us from sin and make us right with God. Here you can help your children understand another important theological word: incarnation. They no doubt know that a *carnivore* eats meat (or flesh). They may have heard of chili *con carne*, chili that is not beans alone but beans with meat (or flesh). Jesus is God in*carnate*—in flesh. The incarnation was when the perfect Son of God took on human flesh to be born as a baby and to grow up to be our Savior. Children have a natural love for all things to do with Christmas. Take advantage of that to teach them theology. As you sing Christmas carols together (and don't do this only at Christmastime!), stop to be sure they understand the words in them and the rich truths they celebrate. Some of our traditional Christmas carols are the most profoundly theological hymns the church possesses.

Children also need to know *why* the Son, who was perfect and complete as God, had to become man in order to save his people. The penalty for sin involves death. In order for the Son of God to save sinners from God's just sentence, he would have to pay the penalty for their sin. He would have to die in their place. God cannot die. The Son of God had to become human if he was going to die to save his people.

Not only that, but, to be our Savior, Jesus would have to be sinless. If he were not, he could not atone for the sins of others. Our Savior had to be born without the sinful nature the rest of us have inherited from Adam, and he had to remain sinless for a lifetime. Because Jesus was conceived by the Holy Spirit, he was born without sin. Because he has all the power and holiness of God, he was able to do what none of the rest of us, not even Adam or Eve, originally sinless, has ever done. Jesus was able to resist every temptation he ever faced and end his life on earth as sinless as on the day he began it. Imagine, with your children, what it would be like to be one of Jesus' siblings, or Mary or Joseph. Imagine living with an infant, toddler, boy, teen who never, ever did or said anything sinful, and who never even had a bad attitude. Consider together your sins of this very day: the things you've said and done and wished you hadn't, the things you should have done and didn't, and the thoughts and attitudes you've had that didn't glorify God. Multiply these by every day of your life and marvel together at the power and the holiness of the Lord Jesus Christ, who resisted every one of those and never gave in to a single temptation.

Things to Know

- Jesus is the Son of God.
- The Son of God is eternal.
- The Son of God willingly became man to save God's people.
- Jesus has all the attributes God has.
- Jesus' human life began when he was begotten by the Holy Spirit and conceived in Mary his mother.
- Jesus is 100 percent human and 100 percent divine.
- Jesus is God incarnate—God in the flesh.
- The Son of God became man to die in the place of his people.
- Jesus was perfectly sinless.

WHAT HE DID

The area of theology that contemplates the Lord Jesus Christ speaks of the person of Christ (who he is) and the work of Christ (what he has done). To consider the work of Christ we consider what he came to earth to accomplish. The short answer to what Jesus has done, and the one he himself referred to often, is that he came to do the will of the Father (John 6:38). It was his Father's good pleasure to bring glory to himself and to the Son through saving sinners ruined by Adam's fall. In order to do this, Jesus had to accomplish two things for his people: he had to remove the great obstacle to peace between them and God—their sin with the justly deserved wrath of God it incurs—and he had to provide for them the perfect obedience God requires of them.

The work of Jesus depends entirely on the person of Jesus. Jesus could only do what he did to save his people because of who he is. Because he is almighty, holy God, he could live a human life of continuous moral perfection. He could resist every attack of Satan to the uttermost, until, every time, Satan had to withdraw to wait for another opportunity. Christ had the strength he needed to bear all the weight of the wrath of God at the accumulated sin of his people. And because he is infinite God, Christ could do these things not for just one person or for two, but for the countless multitudes in heaven described in John's Revelation. Because Jesus is human, he could represent his people. He could experience, as a human, the same temptations that Adam and all of his children experience—and he could resist them all. As a human, he could step into the place of humans, having all their sins laid upon him, and suffer the wrath of God in their stead.

We dread suffering of any kind for our children. Nonetheless, we long for the day, painful as they will find it, when our children feel the darkness and sin of their own hearts and realize how helpless they are to do anything about it. Without the despair such a vision brings, our children will never trust themselves completely to Christ, and without that, they will have no true salvation. The thing is, even when our children have fled, dismayed, to Christ and have found relief by putting their trust in him alone, they will discover that the dark vision of their sin is a recurring one. After a heart has been changed so that it hates the sin it once loved, the owner of that heart will never again enjoy the blissful ignorance he once had. Christians know their sins are forgiven. They know they've been reconciled to God. They go along, rejoicing in that knowledge, all being well until, suddenly, something forces them to take note again of their hearts. As they do, they find deep, dark sin still lurking there. They watch, horrified, as that sin rises up once more and they do (or say or think) things they would like to have thought themselves finished with forever. Despair will roll in. They will feel certain that God must be angry over such moral failure. They will fear that he will surely withhold his love now. They will wonder if, in fact, that salvation experience in their past never really happened at all. It is in these moments of discouragement about the condition of their souls that our children will most need to have been well taught concerning the person and the work of Christ. "Crises in faith often stem," writes Goldsworthy, "from a failure to comprehend the perfection of Christ's person and work and his power to save to the uttermost."[3] We do a great service now for our future, adult Christian children when we ground them in a solid understanding of Jesus as perfect God and perfect man, obedient to every command of God *and* draining every last drop from the cup of God's wrath, both done in our place. When they understand these things clearly, our children can breathe the deep sigh of relief that comes from grasping that their standing with God has nothing to do with their own moral rectitude or lack of it. It depends entirely on Christ, who is perfect, and on what he has done, which lacks absolutely nothing.

Things to Know

- Jesus came to earth to do the will of his Father.
- Jesus obeyed God perfectly in his people's place.
- Jesus died in his people's place, to take the penalty for their sin.
- When our trust is in Jesus, we know we have been saved perfectly and completely.

PROPHET, PRIEST, AND KING

One helpful way to consider what Christ has done for us is to see him in the roles of prophet, priest, and king, the three main leadership roles of God's Old Testament people. As the Westminster Shorter Catechism puts it, "As our redeemer, Christ is a prophet, priest, and king in both his humiliation and his exaltation."[4] This means that Jesus fulfilled those roles for us while he was here on earth and fulfills them now, while he is in heaven, as well.

The Old Testament prophets spoke and wrote God's Word at his command. They communicated to God's people what God wanted them to know about himself, and what his will for them was. The Bible tells us that Jesus is, himself, the Word of God. His is the claim to greatest prophet of all. Jesus said that to see him was to see the Father. When Jesus taught, people marveled at the authority of his teaching. No wonder.

3. Ibid.
4. Douglas Kelly and Philip Rollinson, *The Westminster Shorter Catechism in Modern English* (Phillipsburg, NJ: Presbyterian and Reformed Publishing Company, 1986), 8.

Others taught what they had heard or read. Jesus taught what he, as God, had seen and knew. Not only did Jesus show us the Father and teach about him, Jesus also chose and taught twelve men, then tasked them with writing down his teachings and the story of his life, death, and resurrection, and with taking that information into all the world. In this way, continuing generations of God's people, in all parts of the world, could know God through Christ.

Not only do we now have our perfect prophet's provision of the New Testament, but also that same prophet makes God's will known to us by giving his people the Holy Spirit. The Holy Spirit is the one who gives understanding to God's people as they read his Word. He opens the eyes of their spiritual understanding so they "get" it. He gives them the power they need to carry out God's will once they know it. In the world our children live in, other cults and religions claim to have prophets who reveal truth from God. Many people claim that truth cannot be known, and others claim there isn't any truth to be known in the first place. Only the Holy Spirit can convince our children, born blinded by sin, that Christ is who he says he is. Only the Holy Spirit can create faith in their hearts. Once that faith is there, though, our children will find it strongly buttressed by their knowledge of who it is—the Word of God himself—who has spoken and taught the things they believe.

Early in the history of God's relationship with his Old Testament people, God made a covenant with his people at Mount Sinai. The Israelites' part of the covenant included keeping God's laws for moral behavior as well as following his rules for worship. God put into place for them an elaborate system of priests and sacrifices, in which every worship detail was regulated and every regulation required faithful attention. In this way, God made clear to sinful people that they can only come to him in the way he ordains. Only magnificent grace on the part of a holy God gives sinners access to him at all; certainly, they must come in the way he ordains, not casually, not however they please, not as though they do him a favor in coming. So for centuries, only the priest entered the Holy of Holies, once a year, and then for the purpose of making atonement for the sins of God's people. Ordinary people brought their sacrifices to priests, laid their hands on the heads of those sacrifices before they were killed, then watched as the priest offered them to cover their day-to-day sins. In this way, God taught his people that their sins had earned his judgment of death and that, as long as those sins remained unjudged and unpunished, they barred the way into God's presence. It was in this context that Jesus came as perfect priest and perfect sacrifice. Having never sinned, he stepped into the place of God's people to die instead of them. His sacrifice was the one that all the earlier ones, involving animals, had pictured. He died, rose again, and ascended into the presence of God. There he remains as perfect priest, making intercession constantly for his people and making sure that his people receive every blessing his obedience and sacrifice have earned for them. God's people have a perfect priest who has offered a perfect sacrifice that fully atoned for every sin they will ever commit. The comfort of this assurance is one that will grow on our children as they grow in Christ, since, in greater maturity comes greater awareness of sin and need.

Because God's people are sinful and weak, they have always needed a perfect leader. They require a king to rule them, unruly as they are when left to themselves, and to defend them against their powerful enemies. God gave his Old Testament people kings, but their righteousness and their power were limited. Some were better than others at leading in righteousness or in conquering enemy nations, but none was the king the people needed most. Jesus came, announcing that the kingdom of God had come. He healed the sick, raised the dead, commanded storms, and cast out demons to demonstrate that he was the one who ruled at the center of God's kingdom. When he died, he destroyed the power sin and Satan had held over his people since the fall (Col. 2:13–15). When he rose, he destroyed the power of death, and, one day, he will destroy death itself forever (1 Cor. 15:20–26).

You will probably die before your children do. Have you prepared them so that, as Paul wrote, they "may not grieve as others do who have no hope" (1 Thess. 4:13)? I remember watching by my own father's hospital bed as he lay dying. I thought how lonely it must be to die, and it made me sad that I couldn't help him. The words of Jesus, king of all, came to my mind, bringing comfort that has stayed ever since: "Fear not, I am the first and the last, and the living one. I died, and behold I am alive forevermore, and I have the keys of Death and Hades" (Rev. 1:17–18). Jesus went through death and came out safely on the other side. He goes with his children through their dying. He decides exactly when each one shall die; he holds the keys.

All power belongs to our king. He has the power to change the hearts of those he calls through his gospel so that they cease to rebel against God and desire him instead. This is what will give our children courage to reach out to others and to use their gifts in Christ's service: their king will do what they cannot. He will subdue hearts and draw them to himself as our children serve him. King Jesus rules the hearts of our believing children as well, restraining the sin that yet remains and aiding them in their fight against it. He sits at the right hand of God, ruling all things for the good of his people, the church (Eph. 1:20–23).

As you read Old Testament stories with your children, you will frequently encounter prophets, priests, and kings. Each time, consider God's gracious provision for his people in providing these leaders. Help them to notice how this particular person in this particular office helped prepare the way for the Messiah God was promising. Then consider with them how, no matter how wonderful this particular prophet or priest or king was, he failed. In some way, maybe in many ways, he let down the people of God. Contrast that Bible character with the Lord Jesus Christ, perfect prophet, priest, and king, and list the things he can do for his people that the story's character could not.

Things to Know

- Prophets gave God's word to his people.
- Jesus is the greatest and final prophet.
- Jesus showed God to his people because he is God.
- Jesus speaks God's Word to his people now through the Bible.
- Priests offered sacrifices for the people's sin.
- Jesus offered himself as the perfect and final sacrifice.
- Jesus still intercedes for his people in heaven.

- Kings led and protected God's people.
- Jesus is the perfect, sinless king who defeats all his people's enemies.
- As our king, Jesus rules our hearts and rules the universe for his people's good.

HOW IT ALL HELPS

An accurate understanding of who Jesus Christ is and what he has done offers, to a believing heart, an almost endless set of answers in life's difficulties. Below are only a few examples of the encouragement our adult Christian children will have if they clearly grasp the Bible's teaching about its central figure.

Our children will sometimes fall back in revulsion as they witness the horrors of others' sins or of their own. They can know that Jesus, perfectly holy, knew a much deeper disgust at sin as he lived thirty-three years among sinners, and then actually took the sins of his people upon himself to carry them to the cross. When they face the dismay of seeing themselves sin yet again, or as they help a believing loved one through repeated relapses in overcoming a tough temptation, our children can know that their standing with God the Father is as secure as if they had never sinned, because its basis is what *Christ* has done to please him, not what they do. They can know that, since the one who died for them was fully God, he knew every sin each of us would ever commit. He will never be surprised (as we often surprise ourselves) by some new or recurring sin. He knew we would commit that particular sin, and he knew how many times we would commit it, at the very moment he hung, dying, on the cross for us.

One of the hardest things about pain and suffering is the isolation it creates around the sufferer. Having expressed sympathy upon hearing of someone's trial, the rest of the world then goes on about its business, sympathetic and concerned, but lacking time to consider too deeply another's trouble. Even when help is offered, the helper can only go so far in sharing the sufferer's burden. At the end of the day, pain and heartbreak leave us alone in our misery. If we have taught them well, however, we can rest in the assurance that our believing children will know they are not alone. They will know their Christology well enough to know that Jesus was fully human and faced suffering as fully as they are facing it right now. Jesus knew misunderstanding, even hatred for no cause. He was persecuted, to the point of physical assault and execution. He endured intense physical pain and death, with the added burden of an audience comprised of those he loved, whose anguish he would have witnessed, and of those who mocked and found entertainment in his sufferings. This Christ, who loves his people supremely and who knows precisely how it feels to suffer as a human, is omnipresent God, present with those he loves through every moment of their suffering.

Jesus knew the supreme isolation felt by one in deep anguish. No one understood what was happening as he hung on the cross. Most of his loved ones fled in concern for themselves and left him to suffer alone. His enemies, who were many, mocked, and God the Father himself turned away from him. While our children may sometimes *feel* forsaken by God, Christ knew what it was to have God actually turn his back on him in judgment as he suffered for our sin. Whenever our children must suffer, they will find strong support when they clearly know who Jesus is and what he did for them. He has suffered far more than they ever will, and (supreme comfort!) it was for love of them that he willingly endured such suffering. Whatever the reason that pain, suffering, persecution, or grief have come into their lives, it is *not* because Jesus does not love them, and neither are they alone as they endure.

Not only does Jesus love his people so much that he suffered in their place, since he is divine, he loves with a love that is infinite. It will never end. Nothing can strain it to the breaking point. He has promised to keep those who are his forever, and he is able and willing to do exactly that.

Things to Know

- No sin of ours will ever take Jesus by surprise.
- Because Jesus is fully human, he understands our sufferings.

- Because Jesus is fully God, he is always with his people in all their sufferings.
- On the cross, Jesus was forsaken by God so that his people never would be.
- Jesus will love and keep his people forever—no matter what!

COMING AGAIN IN GLORY

In spite of the insecurities that nag and whisper deep inside of each individual soul, modern mankind likes to tell itself that it's getting better all the time. One day in the future, humanity will suddenly wake up and notice that it has arrived. In truth, though, we might do better to listen to the nagging insecurities from within because they describe us as we are, not as we wish we were. A Christian truth we will want our children to grasp is the truth of Christ's return. There *is* hope for the future, and it is sure and steadfast. It is not, however, based on people and their progress, but on Christ's promise to return and to lead his people into a new heaven and a new earth where righteousness will dwell forever. A solid, foundational assurance of this truth can give courage to our believing children in any situation. When the bad guys win—as they seem to do every day—when the darkness goes on and on and on with the sun never rising, when our children come face to face with death or war or persecution or unimaginable pain in whatever form, they can rest on Christ's promise that it will not always be like this. History has a goal, and Christ our king leads all things to that goal, steadily, relentlessly, come what may. That goal will prove to be the best thing possible for God's glory and for the good of his creation.

Even very young children realize there are problems in our world that need to be fixed. They can think of examples from the playground where disagreements arise or bullies harass their playmates. You can remind them of people they know who have illnesses or disabilities that aren't getting better, or of real life situations of genuine sadness that need to be resolved. Children know they have specific sins they struggle with, and they probably realize what some of yours are as well. When Christ returns, all these things will be settled, once and for all.

In A. A. Milne's *Winnie-the-Pooh* series, the loving mother Kanga gave her little Roo daily doses of "strengthening medicine" so he would grow up big and strong. There is no strengthening medicine like a full-orbed knowledge of Christ. Jesus defined eternal life itself as knowing God the Father and knowing Jesus Christ, whom he has sent (John 17:3). A strengthening medicine such as this will fortify the hearts and minds of our children no matter how difficult the trials or how powerful the enemies that threaten to undo them.

Things to Know

- Jesus will return.
- Jesus will create a new heavens and a new earth where there will be only righteousness.
- God's goal—his glory and the good of his people—will be accomplished.

8

Salvation: What Must I Do to Be Saved?

Many children who have grown up in Christian homes—indeed, many adults—assume they are Christians, but it's not because they clearly understand the truths of the gospel. Rather, they base their assumption on an experience they remember having. They walked down an aisle or they "made a decision" or they prayed a particular prayer; so they are Christians. They are certain they are right with God and will go to heaven when they die. As adults who love God and who love the children in our lives, we may be part of the problem. We're eager to know *our* children are also *God's* children. We may try to make it so easy for children to be saved that we offer them a simple formula, almost like a magic incantation ("Just ask Jesus into your heart"; "Just pray this prayer after me") when what we should offer is the truth of God's Word, communicated as clearly—but also as fully—as we know how and repeated often, with the results left up to God the Holy Spirit.

THE GOSPEL NEEDED

For starters, our children need to know what salvation is and why they need it. They need to learn, early, that Christian doctrine teaches a God who is not inside us, as much of the world around them says, but who stands outside of us, having created us and everything else, and who cannot be known apart from his own revelation. They need to know that this God requires his human creatures to live up to his standards, but we all fail to do so. If our children grow up understanding these things, we can hope they will not entertain our age's common view of spirituality, the one that preaches that everything anyone needs can be found inside the self. Such a view sees no need for salvation from the outside. Indeed, the common view of man's spirituality would be offended at the mere idea.

Children should learn, early on, that the good God created a good world for good human beings, but neither the humans nor the world stayed good for long. Adam and Eve's disobedience in the garden filled the world with difficulties and filled human beings with sin. God did not create us to live in a state of sin, so sin makes us miserable and places us in grave danger. All this may seem obvious. But our culture has so divorced the idea of God from the holiness that is his defining attribute and the sin that is our most devastating problem that we need to be sure the idea of *salvation* makes sense to our children.

You can help your children to understand the concept of salvation by providing them with smaller, simpler examples of situations where people would want someone to rescue them. If I have wandered, lost, for hours in a raging blizzard, I am miserable! I am cold; I am exhausted; I am hopeless. And I am in grave danger. I will freeze to death if someone does not save me from this situation. When Lassie comes bounding up to me through the snow, leading rescue workers who have been searching for me, I am saved from the misery and the danger I was in. I'm taken to warmth, nourishment, shelter. With a grateful pat on Lassie's head from my hospital bed, I say, "That dog was my salvation!" When the villain has tied Mary to the train tracks and the train whistle can be heard in the distance, Mary is miserable with fear and faces a very real danger. When John rides up, cuts the ropes, and snatches her up in his arms just before the train arrives, Mary smiles and says, "You saved me!" As both scenarios demonstrate, we can tell our children, salvation is rescue from a situation that is dangerous and miserable; it includes making the one rescued both safe and happy.

Children will quickly grasp the *danger* of sin. Sin displeases God, and he will judge it. (Although, again, children need to be learning this well as they grow because, probably even before they leave our homes, they will hear a legion of voices mocking the barbaric superstition of a God who judges.) The *misery* of sin, though, may not be as readily obvious to them. The children I teach respond quickly to "What's dangerous about sin?" but they do not have so ready an answer for "What's miserable about sin?" Sin has become so natural to us all that we fail to realize how miserable it makes us. Help your children to think through the aftermath of their actions when they do what they know is wrong. How do they feel, deep inside where no one else sees? What consequences arise from their wrong actions? How are relationships strained and uncomfortable when someone acts out selfish attitudes? People were not created to live this way. The misery of sin lies in its power to enslave us, so that we do, over and over, the very things that keep us miserable. Children need to understand that the Bible teaches that they, like all other human beings, were born sinners. The sin inside enslaves them and makes them enemies of God.

Our children also need to know that they cannot save themselves. No walk down an aisle, no decision made, no prayer repeated, no resolution to be a better person can save them. From inside a great fish deep in the sea, Jonah prayed, "Salvation belongs to the Lord" (Jonah 2:9). Impossible as it was for Jonah to deliver himself from the stomach of a fish and then from the depths of the sea, it is even more impossible for us to deliver ourselves from the misery and danger of sin. Jonah could not even help God save him; God would have to do it all for him. So it is with us. Our children must grow up knowing that salvation is far too great a task for any human. God alone can do all that's needed to save a soul from sin.

Things to Know

- The true God is known only through the Bible.
- God created a good world with good people.
- The first humans disobeyed God and brought sin into the world.
- Salvation is a rescue from danger and misery.
- Sin's danger is God's wrath.
- Sin's misery is in its results and its power over us.
- Only God can save sinners from the danger and misery of sin.

THE GOSPEL PROVIDED

Adam and Eve ate the fruit and plunged God's glorious creation into sin and death. This disaster, great as it was, did not take God by surprise. He had planned salvation long before the need for it arose. When your children contemplate lesser disasters—devastating, to be sure, but not so devastating as the sin from which all devastation comes—there should be comfort in the awareness that no disaster takes God by surprise. As soon as Adam and Eve looked up from the wreck they had made of the world God had given them, God was already promising them a Savior (Gen. 3:15). When the time was right, God sent his own Son to be born of a woman, fully God and fully man.

In the previous chapter, we considered who Jesus Christ is and what he did when he came to earth. That is all part of a thorough understanding of the gospel's message. To the degree that any of us, including our children, understand the person and the work of Jesus Christ, to that degree we have a deeper assurance of our salvation and a greater grasp of the glory of our God. The core of the provision that God made for us in Christ is that Jesus came to do what we could not. He came to restore what sin had ruined. He came to set us right again with the God we were made to enjoy and glorify. In the place of his people, Jesus lived a life of perfect obedience to every one of God's laws; then, also in their place, he died for all the times those laws were broken. *If children do not clearly understand these truths, it is not likely that they possess salvation.*[1]

Things to Know

- God was not surprised by sin.
- God promised a Savior and sent his Son to be that Savior.
- Jesus lived a life of perfect obedience in his people's place.
- Jesus died for sin in his people's place.

1. I qualify this by saying "it is not *likely*" because I do believe the Holy Spirit is capable of working salvation in the hearts of those whose intellectual abilities will never be such that they can grasp and explain back theological truth; however, the pattern of the New Testament leads us to expect that, ordinarily, people will hear, understand, and embrace doctrinal truth as a prerequisite to repentance and faith.

THE GOSPEL OFFERED

The gospel presented in the New Testament calls people to repentance and faith. It does not call people to make a decision for Christ or to ask Jesus into their hearts. It commands people to repent and believe (Mark 1:15). There is salvation only in the one whom God sent as Savior (Acts 4:12), so we must trust in him alone to save us from the sin that has ruled us. And since we are turning to him to save us from sin, we cannot continue to embrace it. We must repent, both of the sin we inherited from Adam, and from the personal, individual sins we have committed in our lifetime.

"What is repentance unto life? Repentance unto life is a saving grace, by which a sinner, being truly aware of his sinfulness, understands the mercy of God in Christ, grieves for and hates his sins, and turns from them to God, fully intending and striving for a new obedience."[2] Such repentance will necessarily be imperfect. It will not ensure the avoidance of sin from now on. In fact, the Christian way of life is, among other things, a life of repentance, turning again and again from sin as it is discovered. Such repentance must be present, however, or true conversion has not occurred.

You sometimes hear this question and answer in Christian counseling circles: "When is a thief not a thief? When he stops stealing? No, when he starts working for his money and begins to share with others."[3] True repentance is more than feeling bad about sin or even ceasing to do a sinful activity; it involves an about-face, with a new intention to do the opposite, God-honoring behavior. I illustrate repentance with children in Sunday school by asking one child to get up from her seat, walk around the room, and return to her chair, asking a second child to get up and walk to the door, and asking a third child to get up, walk halfway to the door, then turn on his heel and return to his chair. "Which best illustrates repentance?" I ask, and, if I've explained the term to them, they choose

2. Douglas Kelly and Philip Rollinson, *The Westminster Shorter Catechism in Modern English* (Phillipsburg, NJ: Presbyterian and Reformed Publishing Company, 1986), 19.

3. Based on Ephesians 4:28: "Let the thief no longer steal, but rather let him labor, doing honest work with his own hands, so that he may have something to share with anyone in need."

the third. The gospel in the New Testament calls for repentance, an about-face, a complete turnaround. It also calls for faith in Jesus Christ.

"What is faith in Jesus Christ?" asks the Westminster Shorter Catechism. "Faith in Jesus Christ," comes the reply, "is a saving grace, by which we receive and rest on him alone for salvation, as he is offered to us in the gospel."[4] A short answer, only one sentence, but packed full of precision! Faith is a saving grace. We must have it for salvation, but God gives it freely; we don't muster it up somehow on our own. I've illustrated it this way with children. Imagine a poor man whose beloved wife has been bitten by a poisonous snake. She will die if she does not have the antidote. The man hurries to the only clinic in town that has the rare medicine, only to learn that its astronomical cost soars high beyond anything he could ever pay, even if he took his whole lifetime to earn it. He turns away, grieving. The sympathetic doctor says, "Wait. I will give it to you for free." The man opens his hand to receive the antidote. But then the doctor says, "But where's your gold cup? Did you not know you can only receive this medicine in a cup made of the finest, purest gold? Otherwise, it loses its potency." Again, the husband turns away, even more disappointed than before. "Never mind," the doctor answers. "I own a golden cup. You may have mine." He hands the husband the cup of pure gold, then pours the medicine into it. So God gives us salvation for free because we could never earn it. We must receive it by faith, however, and we have no faith on our own; so God works in us the faith as well, a gift as free as salvation itself.

By faith, "we receive and rest on [Jesus Christ] alone for salvation." It is not Jesus plus our good works, plus our trying really hard to please God, plus anything. We receive Jesus Christ alone for salvation, and we rest on him alone, all our lives, for our right standing with God. Our children will struggle with doubts. They will wonder: are they really Christians or not? Did they really mean that profession at camp that summer or not? What we should not tell them then is, "Sure you're a Christian, honey. Remember when you (went forward/told Mommy you'd asked Jesus into your heart/prayed to receive Jesus)?" We will want them to understand

---

4. Kelly and Rollinson, *The Westminster Shorter Catechism*, 19.

that what they did or didn't do in the past, or how "real" it was, is not the issue. Right now, today, on what or on whom are they resting for salvation? What are they trusting, right now this minute, to make them right with God? Is it Jesus alone? That is the issue; that is what matters.

Our catechism answer cautions us that we must "receive and rest on Him . . . as He is offered to us in the gospel." To cling in faith to ideas of God we've made up or we've learned from someone else who has not taken them from Scripture is to "receive and rest on" what can do nothing for us. Today I saw a bumper sticker featuring a drawing of a bearded man with a head covering, and the name "Jesus." "It's not *what* you know," the bumper sticker read. "It's *who* you know." Agreed; but the only way to know Jesus is through the book God provided, where the good news, the gospel, is spelled out as God gave it. There is no getting around learning the "what" if we want to know the "who."

The gospel message tells children they are sinners whose sin places them in desperate danger and need. It tells them that God has graciously provided a Savior to obey in their place and then die for their sin. To present this message and then tell a child to "ask Jesus into your heart" is to change the subject. The response the gospel requires is faith—in Christ as Savior—and repentance, with a consequent commitment to obeying Jesus as Lord.

Things to Know
- The gospel requires repentance and faith in Christ.
- Repentance is turning from sin to obey God.
- Faith in Christ is "receiving and resting on him alone for salvation."
- Saving faith is a gift of God's grace; it can never be earned or deserved.

THE GOSPEL APPLIED

God the Father gave God the Son who earned salvation for us by his life of obedience and his death on the cross. The gospel offers Christ as a Savior from sin to anyone who will receive him as such. Those who do are those to whom God the Holy Spirit applies the gospel.

As much as we love our children, we love our God even more. So we want our children to grow up understanding the gospel not as something they can choose if they're wise enough and spiritually minded enough, but as something that displays the power, the grace, and the sovereignty of God as nothing else does. We want to teach our children man's helplessness apart from God's gracious work in the heart. Why does one person hear a gospel sermon and repent in tears and believe while the person sitting right next to her hurries home to fix a sandwich? Because the first person is wiser or more spiritual than the other? No, but because God the Holy Spirit has worked in her heart. He has opened that person's eyes to see her own need and the truth of God's Word, and he has given her spiritual life (which she did not have on her own), making her able to repent and to trust in Christ. This is what Jesus meant when he told Nicodemus, "You must be born again" (John 3:7). If unbelievers are "dead" in trespasses and sins (Eph. 2:1), something must make them alive. The *something* is God (Eph. 2:4–5).

God fully saves his people. He does not provide a perfect way of salvation, then set it before them, hoping they will choose it. He knows they cannot; the very thing they need to be saved from prevents them. Part of the salvation he provides includes making a way for his people to receive it by changing their hearts and bringing them to spiritual life so they can.

My husband helps me show the fourth to sixth graders in our Sunday school class how serious their sin problem is and how desperately they need God's grace in every part of their salvation. He lies across three chairs, perfectly still, pretending he is dead. I tell the children my husband is dead, but I have found a cure for him. I talk to my "corpse," telling him that I hold in my hand a truly "magic" marker (taken from the class supply cupboard). If he will just take it from me and hold it in his hand, it will make him well. When, of course, he does not move, I ask the children, "Why doesn't he just reach out and take it?"

"He's dead," they reply.

I try again. "This magic marker can take care of everything for you," I tell my corpse. No response. "You can trust me; I know what

I'm talking about." Nothing. "You don't believe me, do you?" I turn to the children. "Why won't he believe me?"

"He's *dead*," they insist, a little louder this time.

I make one more attempt. "Look," I tell the corpse, "there's nothing to it. It's so easy. You reach out your hand, you hold this magic marker in it, and you will be alive and well. There's no reason *not* to do it." I pause. "You don't even get it, do you?" I say. "You don't understand what I'm talking about."

Once more I turn to my audience. "There's nothing hard about this, right? Why doesn't he get it?"

"He's *DEAD!*" they repeat, louder still.

And from there it's an easy move to talk about the inability of one dead in sin to reach out and take what God has provided in the gospel, no matter how easy it is. A dead person can do nothing. He cannot believe the gospel; a dead person can't believe anything. He can't understand spiritual truth. A dead person can't understand anything. God must work life in a sinner's heart before that sinner can understand, believe, and receive the gospel.

Older children are fascinated as well by the eerie scene of Ezekiel 37, where the prophet, surrounded by bones dead so long that they lie separated from each other and dried out, is called by God to preach to them. What folly! Preaching to the dried-out bones of dead men! Yet when the prophet preaches, the bones come together and reassemble themselves, even growing new sinews and muscles and flesh. They remain dead, however. God commands the prophet to preach again, and breath (spirit) comes into the dead men, so they rise to their feet, a living army. What a picture of the power of God to use the preaching of his Word to bring spiritually dead people to life.

Things to Know

- Sinners are dead in their sin and cannot repent and believe unless the Holy Spirit enables them by giving them spiritual life.
- God is all powerful in the preaching of the Word to bring new life to sinners.
- The Holy Spirit graciously gives the gifts of repentance and faith.

THE GOSPEL RECEIVED

The gospel is not just for unbelievers. Christians never mature beyond the need to hear the gospel. Rather, they need to hear it over and over because of how it fortifies and empowers them to walk with Christ through all of life. The New Testament epistles were written to believers. In those epistles, the apostles explain, define, and apply the gospel, again and again.

The apostles explain that God justifies those who receive the gospel by faith. The typical reaction of a teacher of children to a word like *justification* is to steer clear of it as being too "adult" to be helpful. Understanding this concept, however, is critical for understanding what the gospel does for us. My favorite question and answer in the Westminster Shorter Catechism is Q&A 33 which asks: "What is justification?" and replies: "Justification is the act of God's free grace by which He pardons all our sins and accepts us as righteous in His sight. He does so only because He counts the righteousness of Christ as ours. Justification is received by faith alone."[5] This definition is both easy to understand and easy to memorize.

I find two illustrations helpful in communicating the concept of justification to children. There is the common legal one, in which we talk about how, in criminal court, a judge or jury decides whether or not the accused has committed the misdeed. If so, they declare him "guilty." If not, they declare him "not guilty." I point out how God does so much more than simply declare us *not guilty*. He declares us *righteous* in Christ, who has been righteous in our place. This will be important to our children, as it is to us, every time they begin to feel that they're failing to do what God requires; they surely must be out of his favor this time. We rest in faith on Christ alone; he has done it all for us.

My other illustration is based on Zechariah's vision of Joshua the high priest, dressed in filthy clothing, standing before the angel of the Lord with Satan beside him to accuse him. The angel had Joshua's dirty garments removed, and then had him clothed in "pure vestments" (Zech. 3:3–5). Consider Cinderella preparing for the ball, I tell chil-

5. Ibid., 10.

dren. While it was nice of the fairy godmother to take away her dirty rags, you need more than that to go to a ball. You need a fancy ball gown—and maybe a pair of glass slippers. The palace guards wouldn't have let Cinderella in just because she wasn't wearing dirty rags. They would expect her to be dressed for the ball. It would never be enough to come before God simply with our sin removed; we must have holy acts of righteousness to present to him. If Jesus had taken away our sins and done nothing else, we still could not come before God. Jesus did more; he clothed us in his own righteousness, so that God accepts us as righteous for Jesus' sake.

Another benefit to those who have received the gospel is *adoption*. God adopts as his children those who believe in the Savior he provided (John 1:12). Those in our culture who still believe in a God of some sort tend to consider all human beings as children of God. The Bible teaches that only those who believe in Christ are God's children, and they have every right and every privilege with God that you would expect a child to have with his father. They may talk with him whenever they like; they may expect that he will provide all they need; they can be confident that they will inherit everything their older brother, Jesus, has earned—and they can assume they will experience their Father's discipline. They must accept such discipline as evidence of their Father's concern for them, and not as punishment.

Believers in the gospel also receive the benefit of sanctification. The Westminster Catechism refers both to justification and to adoption as an "act of grace." These happen once and are complete. The catechism defines sanctification as a "work of grace," because it is not once and for all completed at conversion. It begins then, when God the Holy Spirit sets a person aside to belong to God and to become holy. The process of becoming holy, however, will continue, unfinished, through a believer's whole lifetime. The New Testament writers exhort their Christian readers to apply the gospel by actively using all God has provided to help them to grow in Christlike character. Our children need to understand that sanctification is a process and that God both sanctifies them himself and calls them to take an active part in that process. Otherwise, they will either become discouraged by how slow their progress in holiness seems to be or become nonchalant about diligently pursuing godliness for themselves.

Finally, the apostle Paul tells us that all who have been called and justified will also be glorified (Rom. 8:30). Bodies *and* souls of believers will one day (and for all eternity) experience the perfection of glory God designed them to know. To believe this doctrine is to have boundless comfort for many situations. Neither I, nor those I love, will struggle forever with those sins from which we just can't seem to break free. One day, we will follow our Lord Jesus Christ perfectly, and will be, like him, morally flawless and perfectly holy. If we suffer physically now, or if we're watching a believer whom we love suffer or die, we have the promise of healthy, perfect bodies that will live forever with our Lord.

Timothy Keller explains the apostle Paul's recipe for contentment even when suffering. It is to *think* about the core doctrines of the gospel, like glorification. Whatever we struggle with now, however difficult, is temporary. What we have in Christ is not only greater than any current sufferings, it is eternal. *And* the best is yet to come. We have a future that includes living with Christ in a perfect body and a sinless soul forever. In the context of Philippians, argues Keller, this is what Paul meant when he gave a list of things true, noble, right, etc., calling on his readers to think on those things. It's what he meant when he wrote, "For I consider that the sufferings of this present time are not worth comparing with the glory that is to be revealed to us" (Rom. 8:18). "Our bad things will turn out for good, our good things cannot be taken away, and the best is yet to come," writes Keller. " 'Think on these things' (Phil. 4:8)."[6]

We all realize that mere knowledge of all the right truths will not save our children. A changed heart, that sees and hates its sin and that hungers for Christ, is what they need. The right truths, though, are what God uses to effect that change of heart. A friend gave me this illustration once, which I thought so appropriate. Teaching our children Christian doctrine is like piling up the kindling before making a fire.

6. Timothy Keller, *Walking with God through Pain and Suffering* (New York: Dutton, 2013), 298–301.

The kindling won't catch fire on its own. But the kindling must be there for the flame to ignite. So we teach children doctrine, faithfully piling up firewood, and we pray for God the Holy Spirit to set those truths ablaze in our children's hearts.

Things to Know

- In salvation, God justifies us—forgives our sin and counts Jesus' perfect righteousness as ours.
- In salvation, God adopts us as his children; we can come to him with our needs, and we must trust him when he disciplines us.
- In salvation, God sanctifies us—sets us apart for himself and works in us to make us holy.
- God will one day glorify his saved people—make them perfect in body and spirit.
- What we have in salvation is better than anything we *don't* have in this life and will last forever.

9

The Church: At Home in the Household of God

POPULAR OPINION VS. THE WORD OF GOD

The church has come under harsh attack in our time. Those outside the church have long maintained that they do not need church involvement in order to have valid spiritual experiences. One can worship alone in a beautiful, natural setting just as well (maybe even better), they say, than in a building with walls. In our time, though, even many who profess Christianity have no use for the organized church. They maintain that churches are filled with hypocrites or led by those whose doctrine is hopelessly corrupt. They despair of finding any church leaders worthy of following. If they gather with other believers at all, they do it in "The Church of the Living Room," where decisions and beliefs are based on the consensus of a few like-minded individuals. Or they connect with an electronic church. Even to attend, let alone join, an actual local church that meets regularly in a building is considered unnecessary at best, and possibly even detrimental to one's Christian faith.

The problem with such thinking is that it directly opposes the Bible in general and the New Testament in particular. From the beginning, God's purpose has been to have *a people*, not simply a collection of individual persons, as his own people. We first meet the promise "they shall be my people and I shall be their God" in Genesis, and we can follow it through the entire Bible. (In fact, it can be a worthwhile exercise to use a concordance with children whose reading skills are adequate and trace those words through the Bible. God says them to Abraham, to Moses, to the Israelites in the wilderness, to kings, to prophets—and apostles continue to quote them in their epistles.) To be joined to Christ is to be joined to his church. The entire New Testament calls believers to active involvement in that union. Summarizing God's purpose for his whole creation as described by Paul in Ephesians 3, J. I. Packer writes, "It [the church] is the centerpiece of God's plan to display his mind-boggling wisdom and goodness to all the angelic powers."[1]

Three New Testament metaphors can help to show children how important the church is from the perspective of Christ and his apostles. The first metaphor is that of a bride. The church is Christ's bride (Eph. 5:25–32). Ask your children to think of a story or movie where a man has to do brave and difficult things to earn the right to marry the woman he loves. The prince in the story of Sleeping Beauty has to break the sleeping spell and, in Disney's version, fight the dragon. In *Beauty and the Beast*, the Beast has to find a way to get Belle to love him in spite of his frightful appearance. You can also tell any stories you might have of a male relative or friend the children know who had to meet a protective father's demands or surmount obstacles in order to marry the woman he loved. Christ's love for his bride brought him from the glory of heaven to our broken world, then caused him to give his life in the place of his bride. If we claim to love him, how can we not care about the bride he loves so dearly?

The second metaphor is that of a human body (1 Cor. 12:12–27). The Bible tells us that the church is the body of Christ. Christ is the head. He directs, commands, gives life itself to all the members. They are united under him into one whole, each useless and unable to function if cut off from the rest. To illustrate the importance of each member of Christ's body to the body as a whole, you can give children tasks to accomplish while not allowing them to use specific, necessary body parts. Move an item from the floor up onto a table without using your hands. Travel across a room without moving your legs. Find page 139 in a book while wearing a blindfold. The New Testament tells us that

1. J. I. Packer, *Taking God Seriously: Vital Things We Need to Know* (Wheaton, IL: Crossway, 2013), 92.

God himself has gifted each believer with abilities to use for the benefit of other believers, and has then put them all together into a body. Each member needs the others. Each member is required to minister to the others. The third biblical metaphor is that of a building, intended as a dwelling of the Holy Spirit (Eph. 2:19–22). You can draw a picture of a building with your children, labeling and discussing the importance of a foundation (the teaching of the apostles and prophets), a chief cornerstone (Christ himself), and every single brick (individual believers). What good is a brick when it is all by itself, separate from the rest of the structure?

Things to Know

- God's purpose has always been to have a people for himself.
- God displays his glory through the church.
- The church is the bride of Christ, who loved her and died for her.
- The church is a body whose members need each other and whose head is Christ.
- The church is a dwelling for the Holy Spirit, with each Christian a stone in the building.

WHAT REALLY MATTERS?

While some modern people consider churches unnecessary, or even harmful, others still value the church. They realize, however, that all kinds of churches exist, so they appreciate the need to evaluate any church they're considering attending. Unfortunately, people often use criteria for choosing a church that do not reflect New Testament priorities. Ashamed by the repeated refrain of nonbelievers that churches fight with each other over all kinds of trivia, some people have come to value unity in the face of all differences as the fundamental mark of a true church. And indeed, Jesus did pray that his followers would all be one, as he and the Father are one (John 17:21–23), so that the world would know he had been sent by the Father; however, he prayed this for those who would believe in him through the word of the apostles

(John 17:20). While the church should work diligently to guard the unity of the Holy Spirit, setting aside personal preferences and nonessential differences, the church does not have the luxury of unity at any cost. Her Lord forbids her to maintain fellowship with those who do not hold the basics of New Testament doctrine among their beliefs. The true church preserves, protects, and proclaims the truth of God's Word.

Another legitimate concern among those who still value the church is that she becomes too readily preoccupied with her own concerns, giving far too little attention to the needs of the lost. So another false measure of the value of a church has become that of appeal to nonbelievers. This standard involves asking if a church offers programs and deliberately structures services so that nonbelievers will want to come. And yet, it has become increasingly apparent of late that, when churches make a top priority of attracting non-Christians, they inevitably sacrifice substance in their teaching, leaving the Christians in their midst spiritually undernourished and without the means for growth in Christian maturity. The true church takes seriously Christ's call to teach *all* that he has commanded (Matt. 28:20), and Paul's example of making known the *whole* counsel of God (Acts 20:27).

More recently, contemporary churches have become eager to show the world they have a meaningful mission to fulfill. But that mission has become just different enough from the church's true calling that it, too, has become a misguided standard for measuring a church's validity. What many churches today consider their main mission looks very much like the chosen causes taken up by the rest of the world. In a bid to demonstrate relevance and compassion to a watching world, some churches have redefined their missions in terms of creating programs for the poor, ending human trafficking, providing relief to third-world countries, or doing a number of similar activities that today's world applauds. Of course God cares about all these things. Of course Christians should minister to physical needs as well as to spiritual ones. Of course Christians should demonstrate love to neighbor in whatever way is most appropriate in their particular contexts. But the number one mission of *the church*, given by Christ himself, is one that no other organization or international celebrity will work for, and that is the making of disciples for Christ through the faithful teaching and preaching of the Word of God (Matt. 28:19–20). The true church faithfully proclaims the gospel, calling nonbelievers to faith and building believers in the faith, whether the world approves or whether it doesn't.

The apostle Paul calls the church "the pillar and support of the truth" (1 Tim. 3:15 NASB). The church upholds, teaches, and lives by what God has spoken, which we find in the book where he had it recorded. Sometimes, the culture around us approves what the church believes and proclaims. More often, the culture around us finds that same teaching abhorrent. The church's task is to go on believing and proclaiming God's Word, regardless of the popularity of its message.

Our children may have friends who attend churches that look, to our children, as if they would be much more fun or much more exciting. We will want not only to build into our children the habit of regular church involvement but also to teach them what the New Testament calls the church to be and to do, and to explain to them the reasons why our churches do things the way they do.

Things to Know

- The true church protects and teaches the truth of the Word of God.
- The true church teaches all that Christ has commanded.
- The church's first priority is proclaiming the gospel to nonbelievers and building up believers in the faith.
- The church must remain faithful to God's Word, no matter what outsiders say.

THE CHURCH-PARENT TEAM

I always want a reason for what I do. Having taught children in church settings for decades, it's important to me that there be a good reason for doing so. All of us who teach have met parents who drop their children off for our classes but who clearly never teach them any further at home. With only a few minutes to use once a week, we feel the frustration of trying to ground children in the most important content that exists. We know that this way of teaching Bible and doctrine is not only ineffective; it is not biblical. The Bible directs *parents* to teach their children about God and his Word. In both Old Testament and New, fathers and mothers are specifically called to the responsibility and privilege of teaching their children God's truth. And this teaching is so important that God calls on parents to be teaching it all the time—at home, out and about, when getting up, when going to bed. A few minutes on Sundays will not do the job.

Some people, though, have swung far to the opposite extreme. Insisting that the Bible gives the teaching of children to their parents, they teach that children should never have teachers, including Sunday school teachers, who are not their own parents. To this I would say that the New Testament calls the church to teach and to disciple its people. It does not specify only adult people. The children among us are part of the people the church is called to teach. There are times when teaching will be much more effective when using a vocabulary and teaching on a level that aims at children.

In addition, there is an aspect of discipling children that parents cannot do on their own. The New Testament knows nothing of faithful disciples of the Lord Jesus who do not also love the church. Most of the commands in the New Testament epistles involve relationships between believers in the church. When children grow up without attending church or with little involvement with church members, a big chunk of their discipling is left undone. Only the church can teach children to love the church. As we bring our children on a regular basis, they get to know and love the body of Christ. They have a class where they can gather with friends of the same age for teaching that takes into consideration the needs and characteristics of their age. They find a teacher there who knows them well and keeps track of their concerns and their joys. They find ushers at church who greet them by name when they enter. They meet adults who always recognize and hug them. They may have an adult friend who hands out little treats every Sunday morning when the service has ended. These things go a long way to making our children feel at home in the household of God. There are potlucks where children eat quickly, then go and play while adults visit. There are special holiday services. There are hymns that are frequently sung, becoming a rich shared heritage with the others who sing them. There are friends who invite families into their homes. All these things build for our children a collection of memories that give them a sense of belonging and help them to feel that it is good to be with the Lord's people on the Lord's Day. Parents can teach children that the church is important, and that they should be a part of it. But only the church can make children *want* to be a part of it and give them a sense of truly belonging.

I have been a teacher—of several different subjects—for years. So naturally, I believe in matching the content and the presentation to the capabilities of the audience. Our churches should provide times of teaching specifically for children. We should find ways, in our classes, to arouse the interest of the children. We should use methodologies that work well for them. We should do everything in our power to communicate the riches of God's Word in a way that they, as children, can understand and take to heart. This is not all our churches should be doing with children, though. Many churches plan their services so that, whenever there is an adult worship service, there is also a "children's church" or classes for children. They would say that this accomplishes two things: it enables children to learn and worship in a way they will be able to comprehend, and it enables adults to learn and worship free from distraction. In fact, I visited a church once where the pastor asked parents to please avail themselves of the concurrent children's programs in the same breath in which he asked everyone to turn off their cell phones.

We think children "get more out of" programs for their own age group. They *do* get good teaching they can understand from classes for children of their age, and so churches should provide such classes. However, except for the very youngest infants and toddlers, churches should not provide such classes *at the same time as* the weekly assembling of God's people together as one to worship him. Our children are a part of us. They need to be present when the people of God gather to praise him and to hear his Word proclaimed. There are all kinds of things our

143

children will miss out on if they always leave the church service for a child-oriented presentation.

For one thing, no matter how orderly a children's class or a children's church is, it will never have the solemnity and reverence that a worship service for adults will have. When our children stay with us in church, they learn how to conduct themselves in a worship service. This may not sound important. But I have observed in several different churches the behavior of children (and even teens) who are accustomed only to being with their peers, when, for whatever reason, they *do* attend a worship service. They do not know how to act. They squirm, whisper, whine, slouch, sleep, go in and out for drinks and bathroom visits, and fail to participate in the singing or in active listening to the proclamation of God's Word. It is possible for a child to grow up in a family that attends church every Sunday and reach adulthood without once going to church, because first his children's church, then his youth group met during the church's worship service. Where and when could he have learned appropriate behavior and attitude in worship? Yes, children are children and need ample opportunity to move, jump, run, and make a noise. This is how God designed them. But it will not hurt them at all to spend an hour a week learning to curb their natural inclinations in order to be reverent toward God and thoughtful toward others. If we teach them to participate in worship when they are young, it will be their habit as they grow.

No matter how a children's church service seeks to imitate adult worship, there will be no administration of the sacraments in children's church. The Lord's Table is an essential, Christ-ordained part of the worship of God's people. While children, for the most part, will not participate in it, they can observe how important it is to the people who are most important to them. They can learn how glad and how solemn an activity it is. They can begin to appreciate how important it is by the very fact that this is one time when they are *not* allowed to share in the food being distributed. People will not be baptized in children's church either, and children should grow up observing baptisms, free to ask their questions later, and hearing the teaching of their pastors and parents about what baptism means.

The Bible calls on the church to *teach* its people, and we do that with classes for our children. But the Bible also gives priority to the preaching of God's Word by those set aside as elders and pastors. If children begin a worship service with everyone else, then leave when dismissed right before the sermon, what are they learning about the proclamation of the Word? Are we teaching them that we can't expect children to profit from preaching? Are we communicating that only people of a certain intellectual capacity can benefit from the proclamation of God's Word? Are we teaching them that this part of the worship service is unimportant? Are we teaching them that we expect them to find it boring? Remember that the preaching of the gospel is *always* foolishness to the unconverted, no matter the person's age. Yet it is the preaching of the gospel that God has ordained to work the miracle of rebirth and the ongoing process of sanctification in the hearts of those he calls—no matter their age.

I propose that our churches encourage parents to bring their children with them into worship. They can do this by demonstrating patience and understanding as children learn to sit quietly; children will definitely need time to learn! They can do this by educating the congregation on the value of including children in worship, asking childless adults to be understanding and welcoming to the children in their midst. They can do this by helping those who lead in worship to remember there are children present, explaining the words of a hymn so that children will understand what is being sung, or announcing, before the sermon, something children should listen for in it.

I propose that parents come prepared to spend the extra time and, yes, to give up some of their own ability to concentrate, in order to train their children to worship with God's people. As God's people stand to sing, children can stand with them and a patient adult can teach them to follow along in the hymnbook, using a finger to help the child keep the place. At home, parents can teach children some of the songs most commonly used in their church's worship so that, even if they are too young to read, there will be times when children can sing along because there are songs they know from memory. We can encourage children to listen for certain things during the service, because this will train them to listen with attention. They can listen for what specific persons the pastor prays for in his prayer, and why he prays for them. They can make a mark on a paper every time they hear a certain word in the sermon—"prayer" if that is the day's topic, or "God," "Jesus," etc. Children who are older can be trained to listen to see if the pastor mentions a number (as many pastors do), making a list of what the numbers are: three points to a sermon, or five things we see in this passage, or four commands God gave to Joshua. They can listen for a specific example the pastor gives or for a Bible story (if there is one that day) or for the topic in general, and then draw a picture to illustrate it. (Caution: this isn't drawing just anything in order to keep children quiet; this is deliberate drawing of something heard in the sermon to help children learn to listen.) Older children can be taught to take notes or even make outlines. Will most children *enjoy* this in the sense of finding it fun? Probably not. Do children enjoy going to bed on time or doing their homework or eating their vegetables? Yet we require that they do these things, in the hope that they will form habits that will stand by them in later life, when they appreciate the value of the habits they have learned.

Church involvement, as we see in the New Testament, is much more than simply attending worship on the Lord's Day. It involves fellowship and ministry and caring for one another, so faithful parents will want to find ways their children can observe and even participate in the church's "body life." Children can help prepare food for church gatherings or for church members who need a meal. They can pray for, and send cards to, those who are sick. They can write letters to encourage missionaries. They can go with their parents to help out at church work parties. They can be involved in many ways with the people of God and, as they are, they come to feel that the family of God is *their* family. It is where they belong. Such a sense of belonging will provide them with family wherever they go, anywhere in the world, as long as they are on this earth, and throughout eternity as well. It will also provide them with the perspective on the church that is the New Testament's perspective: Christ loves the church and is joined to her, and he gives every individual believer the privilege of being joined to her as well.

Things to Know

- Children can and should participate in the church's worship.
- Children can and should hear the preaching of God's Word.
- There are many ways to encourage children to participate creatively and constructively in church worship services and activities.

10

God's Law: Walking in the Truth

Simple awareness of and even assent to biblical content and doctrinal truth does not equal the faithful discipleship we long to see in our children. As the apostle John said of his children in the faith, so we say both of our own children and of those we have taught: "I have no greater joy than to hear that my children are walking in the truth" (3 John 4). Our children must embrace the truths we teach and love and trust the God those truths reveal. First, though, the doctrinal truths and the Bible content must be there to embrace. Before our children will love and trust God, they must know enough about him to see how worthy of love and trust he is.

Once parents have filled young minds with the beauty of the Bible's teaching about God and his world, their task has only begun. Parents will need to model, by their own lives, the beauty of a life lived by this teaching. They will need to train their children to live by God's laws, diligently and without letup, because their children are sinners who will resist in dozens of ways daily. That resistance will provide one opportunity after another to preach the gospel to children, proclaiming both the law and the grace of God. Parenting is a huge job, involving many complex tasks. In acknowledgment of that fact, I've included, at the end of this book, a list of resources that address other aspects of raising children, written by authors well qualified to discuss them. For the most part, though, those tasks fall outside the scope of this book. This book's theme is the priority of right knowledge. For this chapter, too, the chapter most easily recognizable as "practical," the emphasis continues to be on *knowing*. If our children are going to "walk in the truth," they must first know the truth.

The motivation for walking in truth must come from a right knowledge of God. Last night, I watched a panel discussion from Ligonier's National Conference of 2012. Del Tackett commented that university and college campuses are the most hostile places to Christianity in all America. R. C. Sproul responded to this comment by suggesting that a relationship exists between that academic hostility and the great revolution in standards of sexual morality in the last few decades of our country's history. College professors want to continue in their extramarital affairs. College students want the freedom to enjoy sex before marriage. The easiest way to do these things and experience no guilt over doing them is to deny the existence of the God who forbids them.[1] Someone convinced that he lives in the presence of the God of Scripture cannot sin with impunity. Our children must grow up knowing of the sovereign God who tells his creatures, "You shall," and "You shall not." Unpopular as it is, they must know that this God holds every human being accountable for what he or she does, says, and thinks.

One thing that complicates giving our children this critical instruction is the overwhelming consensus of our culture that the only thing we could possibly do that would be truly bad or evil is to say that something someone else is or does is *bad* or *evil*. "Tolerance" has become all-important, and it no longer means civility toward people themselves while refusing to accept or like their viewpoints or actions. It now means cheerful acknowledgment that they are just as right in holding those opinions and just as good in carrying out those actions as anyone else is. In common parlance, most of us—including the children and teens I know—have come to see this as just "being nice." It simply isn't good manners to say that what someone else believes or does is wrong. So we hold "values" instead of moral absolutes. Based on what we as Christians believe from the Bible, we may consider certain behaviors *inappropriate* (a word I hear from my teen students enough to have become weary of it), but we would never tell the person doing the behavior that the behavior is actually wrong. All this is bad enough when it comes to a biblical presentation of the gospel; after all, if no belief or behavior is wrong, there is no sin; if there is no sin, why would we need a Savior from

1. "Questions & Answers #2," *The Christian Mind: 2012 National Conference*, DVD (Orlando: Ligonier, 2012).

it? But as our children grow up breathing in the air of tolerance and values, they will lose their own moral compass if they do not learn that God's law is absolute, whether or not humans *value* it. At our children's own moments of powerful temptation to do what God forbids, when everyone else says, "Aw, that's not really wrong," they need to understand that God does in fact forbid it, and it is his opinion that counts supremely.

The world in which our children are growing up seeks to silence God in every area where he has spoken in moral terms. It tells our children that, if there is a God, he is only there to love and to help. He has no stringent requirements; he understands and accepts our behavior as it is. Our contemporaries would tell us that, even if it were possible to do something God disapproves of (and they really don't think it is since he lovingly understands everything we do), he would forgive. This is especially true in areas of sexual morality. People need sexual intimacy, our culture insists, and, if they want to be healthy, they need to have it, whether they're married or not. As for people who *are* married, God wants them to be happy, say our contemporaries. If they're not happy in their marriage, they need to leave it and try another, or live with someone without marrying. God, if there even is such a being, won't mind. As for gender differences, our culture's consensus is that there are none, only accidents of biology. If, therefore, you are a male and want a male spouse, or if you are a female and want a female spouse, or if you want to change the gender you were born with—why not? Why would God care? Teaching and raising children in this environment will require wisdom and grace. To maintain God's standards of sexual purity in our current culture is to be considered as a killjoy at best, as mean, hateful, and prejudiced at worst. Yet our children need to grow up learning God's standards, clearly delineated in his Word, while also understanding the doctrines that touch on these things. *All* sin—not just certain sins—is ugly and abhorrent to God, including our own sins and those of our children. We are all sinners and need God's grace. God calls us to love sinners by helping them to see that they are sinners in order to help them understand God's provision for sin.

Another area in which our culture's idea of right and wrong directly opposes the teaching of Scripture is in upholding a culture of the self as all-important. Consider how important words like *self-esteem, self-promotion, self-help,* and *self-expression* have become to counselors, popular books and magazines, talk shows, and school curricula. In the thinking of our culture, whatever *can* be done for one's self *should* be done for one's self. The error or fault would be in refusing to put oneself first. Our Lord specifically taught, by word and by example, that God and his requirements come before anything, including the self. A true disciple is one who *dies* to self, sacrifices self, forgets self, denies self. As David Wells points out, such "self" words as *self-discipline, self-sacrifice, self-restraint,* or *self-abasement* ring out like obscenities to the ears of our contemporaries. Like the current notion of tolerance, the concept of self as supreme permeates our society, and our children will need to be shown the contrast of the New Testament's teaching about self with that of our culture's.[2]

Therefore, one content area we must include as we teach children is the content of God's law. Children should learn the Ten Commandments, and we should supplement that learning with the full-bodied teaching of the catechisms on what those commandments require, in their positive aspects (what we should do) as well as in the negative (what we should not do). Children must grow up learning the high standards Jesus sets for his followers in the Sermon on the Mount and in other parts of his teaching. They should hear, repeatedly and often, the teaching of the apostles in their letters on what Christians must be and do. At the same time, they must be convinced of the liberating truth of the gospel, supplying us with grace for all the times we fail, and with power for all the things God calls us to do that we could never do on our own.

You can illustrate the discord between God's Word and our culture's messages by playing an audio recording of Scripture while simultaneously playing a piece of modern music or a recorded discussion. Be sure that the Scripture audio is played relatively softly. Have your children suggest how the competing voices of modern society attempt to silence or drown out the voice of Scripture from their hearing. Ask them for ideas on what they can do to make sure they're giving God and his Word the attention they should.

2. David Wells, *The Courage to Be Protestant: Truth-Lovers, Marketers, and Emergents in the Postmodern World* (New York: Wm. B. Eerdmans Publishing Co., 2008), 170.

One way to pay attention to God is to think often of who God is and what he has done for us. Timothy Keller points out the spiritual significance of the Bible's meaning of *remember* and *forget*. He notes that when biblical authors ask God to remember his lovingkindness or to not remember their sins, they aren't supposing that God actually forgets things. They are asking God to act toward them in such a way as would be in keeping with his lovingkindness, and to not act toward them in a way that would be in keeping with their sin. Similarly, Keller writes, when the Bible speaks of God's people forgetting him, it means that, though they know all about God and his requirements, they have ceased to allow what they know in their heads to influence their feelings, their choices, and their actions. For us, too, Keller writes (and for our children, I might add), this forgetfulness leads to an ongoing need for revival. "Our hearts are like a bucket of water on a very cold day," Keller writes. "They will freeze over unless we regularly smash the ice that is forming." The obvious remedy for such deadly forgetting is to reverse it, and to remember. Peter writes that if a Christian is not demonstrating Christlike character, it isn't that he's not trying hard enough; rather, he has "forgotten that he was cleansed from his former sins" (2 Peter 1:9). Peter's solution? "Therefore I intend always to remind you of these qualities, though you know them and are established in the truth that you have" (v. 12). Jesus, too, called on his disciples to eat bread and drink wine together "in remembrance of me" (Luke 22:19).[3] We sometimes hear that we need to "preach the gospel to ourselves," and so we do. We need to continually remind ourselves of what God has done for us in Christ so that we will allow it to affect the thoughts we think and the choices we make. As parents and teachers, we want to be continually doing the same for our children and teaching them to consistently remind themselves of what they know as well.

David Wells makes a strong case for the Western church's steady drift away from biblical Christianity in doctrine and conduct. He urges a return to the beliefs and practices of Reformed theology, what he calls a "renewed Protestantism." To believe and practice once again

3. Timothy Keller, *Judges For You* (Purcellville, VA: The Good Book Company, 2013), 41–43.

153

what the Bible teaches, he writes, would provide "a joyous sense of knowing God . . . through his Son, of being able to live in his world on his terms and celebrating his sovereign rule over all of it." It would enable its adherents to live on God's terms, which are "the terms of fullness, of a growing completeness, of wisdom, and of life." Such a faith "will be sinewy and tough. It will not cave in intellectually to all the fads and rackets of our time. It will have an infectious joy in doing what is right. There will be a sense of awe in God's creation presence, of gratitude in being able to serve him in all the callings he gives."[4] Such a faith requires a clear knowledge of the Bible and of Christian doctrine.

A Christian life can only grow strong when it has roots firmly planted in the truths of the previous eight chapters. A correct understanding of our holy God will give our children a sense of right and wrong, sin and guilt. A right knowledge of God's grace and of the gospel will give them the power and boldness to go out each new day, regardless of yesterday's failures, and begin anew to live faithfully for God's glory. Our children will need to remember these truths and doctrines, allowing them to impact their lives, and not forgetting who God is and what he has done. Our task is to be sure the truths and the doctrines are there for them to remember.

Things to Know

- God is our Creator and king; he tells us what we must do and what we must not do.
- God hates all sin.
- God provides salvation from all sin.
- God gives his law in the Ten Commandments.
- The gospel gives grace for when we fail to keep God's law.
- The gospel gives power to help us keep God's law.
- We must remember who God is and what he has done for us.
- We must make knowing, remembering, and obeying God's Word a top priority.

4. Wells, *The Courage to Be Protestant*, 174.

PART THREE

How to Help Our Children Know

11

Rigor, Reading, Rote, and Balance: Some Foundational How-Tos

EMBRACE RIGOR IN TEACHING

Decades ago, J. Gresham Machen said, "The depreciation of the intellect, with the exaltation of the feelings or of the will, . . . is rapidly leading to a condition in which men neither know anything nor care anything about the doctrinal content of the Christian religion, and in which there is in general a lamentable intellectual decline."[1] Machen was correct then, and this antipathy to all things intellectual in general and to doctrine in particular has only increased in the years since he wrote. In his book *Christless Christianity*, Michael Horton states that Americans possess a "fairly pronounced anti-intellectual streak."[2] The average American leans toward the pragmatic rather than the propositional; we want to *do* something, and what we believe takes a back seat to the doing. "It is often said today that Christians, at least evangelicals, know the truth but do not live it," writes Horton. "Numerous surveys, however, contradict the first premise. In a recent Pew study, for example, evangelical Christians trailed atheists, agnostics, Jews, and Mormons in knowing what Christianity teaches. And as far as knowing *why* they believe it, most cannot articulate anything beyond their

1. Quoted by Michael S. Horton in *Christless Christianity* (Grand Rapids: Baker Books, 2008), 245.
2. Ibid.

personal experience."[3] Consequently, if we would provide our children with a rich, rooted theology by which they may live their whole lives, both church and family must commit themselves to rigorous preaching, teaching, and study, and maintain that commitment. Such a commitment is the first and most foundational "how-to."

The objection that Christianity is a religion for the heart, not for the head, or that teaching doctrine makes proud Christians and divided churches becomes clearly foolish when we squarely face the alternative—*not* teaching doctrine. This would result in the very ignorance described in the preceding paragraph. Will our children love God more if they know less about him? "Ignorance," wrote Cotton Mather, "is the mother not of devotion but of heresy."[4]

How to Know

- Intellectually rigorous preaching, teaching, and study will serve the church and its children well.
- The absence of doctrinal preaching and teaching will ultimately lead people astray.

DEVELOP GOOD READING HABITS

A lifetime of love for the knowledge of God presupposes a lifetime of study, and a lifetime of study requires the ability to read. As appreciation for the intellectual declines, so does the value set upon reading. We live in a time when "image is everything." Most people's information comes to them through images, usually on screens of some sort, rather than through written words. Even though some of those screens provide us with things to read, those very screens have changed the way we take in information, and, consequently, the ways in which we think about anything. A multitude of researchers and writers have commented on these trends.

3. Michael S. Horton, "Conversations for a Modern Reformation," *Modern Reformation*, September/October 2012, 31.

4. Quoted by Joel Beeke in "Profiting from the Puritans for Devotional Reading," Banner of Truth, November 5, 2003, http://banneroftruth.org/us/resources/articles/2003/profiting-from-the-puritans-for-devotional-reading/.

David L. Ulin, author of *The Lost Art of Reading: Why Books Matter in a Distracted Time*, reminds us of how easy it is to check e-mail or Facebook or countless other pieces of information from the Internet. Because it is so easy, all of us are always checking, countless times, all day long. "What am I looking for?" he asks. "Something, everything, a way of staying on top of the information . . . it doesn't matter. The looking is an end unto itself. . . . In a world of endless information . . . we face endless anxiety about our ability to keep up, to maintain a place amid the onslaught, to make sense of all the data and what it means."[5]

Roger Bohn coauthored a study on the enormous amount of information the contemporary American looks at online daily. Bohn's conclusion: "Our attention is being chopped into shorter intervals and that is probably not good for thinking deeper thoughts."[6] And Edward Hallowell, a psychiatrist specializing in Attention Deficit Disorder, says, "We have a generation of people who . . . are so busy processing information from all directions they are losing the tendency to think and feel. [And] much of what they are exposed to is superficial."[7]

Author Tony Reinke points out that using the Internet trains us to skim and to browse where, once, we would have read and reflected. He quotes from an article in *The Atlantic* with the provocative title "Is Google Making Us Stupid?" In it, Nicolas Carr explains how those who keep the Internet working have a strong motive for encouraging us to keep moving when we use it. He explains that, as we surf, we leave "crumbs of data" behind—"the more crumbs, the better" for those who want to trace our interests so they can know what they might be able to sell us. "The last things these companies want," wrote Carr, "is to encourage leisurely reading or slow, concentrated thought. It's in their economic interest to drive us to distraction." Reinke follows up his quotation from the article by writing that reading a book "cannot happen without disciplined and sustained linear concentration. Instead of browsing for

5. David L. Ulin, *The Lost Art of Reading: Why Books Matter in a Time of Distraction* (Seattle: Sasquatch Books, 2010), 76–77.
6. Ibid., 81.
7. Ibid.

fragments of information, we must learn to become deep thinkers who work hard to comprehend."[8]

Obvious as it seems at first, if we want our children to know their Bibles and Christian doctrine well, we must help them develop the ability to read. We will have to teach them, by our own example and by providing them with practice, to read books and to think about what they've read. While it would be counterproductive to forbid them to ever use the Internet, we still want to be sure they also make time to interact with books.

In 1940 (with a later revision in 1972), Mortimer Adler wrote a book whose title seemed so obvious that, at first glance, people may have wondered, "What's the point?" especially considering *when* he wrote it, since the age of information-via-image-and-screen had not yet arrived. The book was *How to Read a Book*, and it gave people timeless tips on how to read a book in such a way that the most important points would be grasped and retained. Practice in learning how to read any nonfiction book well can only serve to improve our Bible reading skills. For, remember, the Bible *is* a book. Like any book, it must be read thoroughly and studied diligently, with care taken to see that the main points of its authors are grasped.

So as you read, whether you are reading the Bible, a commentary, a work of theology—or any nonfiction book, for that matter—practice using at least some of Adler's excellent suggestions, at least some of the time. Train your children (especially your teen children) in how to do this, too. Before beginning to read the book itself, read any short summaries, such as those at the beginning or on the book jacket or in a review. Then go on to read the table of contents. If there is an introduction or a preface, read that. All these things introduce you to the book's basic content and main points. They give you the overall direction in which the author intends to take you and, if you know *where* you're going, it will be much easier to find your way along the journey. Before you actually begin chapter 1, flip through the book, reading all the headings. This, again, gives you an overview that helps you follow

---

8. Tony Reinke, *Lit! A Christian Guide to Reading Books* (Wheaton, IL: Crossway, 2011), 141.

the stepping-stones that will lead you where the author wants you to go. When you are actually ready to begin the first chapter, read the opening paragraph and the last paragraph first—to get your bearings—and, as you progress, notice any places (highlight them or, even better, copy them down) where the author uses "first," "second," "third," or any other means of listing. At the end of each chapter (or each section), stop and summarize in your own words what you've just read to be sure you "got" it. All along the way, stop and think about what your author is saying. Look up from the page and reflect. Ask your questions of him or her, mentally, and consider whether you agree with what was written and, more importantly, whether the Bible agrees with it. Training ourselves and our children to read nonfiction, at least occasionally, in such a time-consuming, labor-intensive manner can only help us and them to become better readers of Scripture, with its profound thoughts and carefully crafted lines of reasoning.

Reading fiction can also strengthen our children's ability to understand Scripture because it exercises their imaginations. Reinke points out that the extensive use of the poetic and the apocalyptic in Scripture relies on the reader's ability to imagine. The book of Revelation, for example, "invites us to see ultimate reality through our imaginations in breathtaking, earth-scorching, mind-stretching, sin-defeating, dragon-slaying, Christ-centered, God-glorifying images that change the way we act think, act, and speak. To view imaginative literature as a genre fit only for the amusement of children is an act of spiritual negligence."[9]

Train your children to read and to think about what they read. Train them to read widely and think deeply. Encourage them to imagine. While some children have a natural love for books, many don't, and the number of those who don't will only increase as image becomes more and more pervasive. But don't give in to the temptation to give up on your nonreader. The poorest reader can improve with practice. You don't want to force your children to sit and read endlessly, as Joseph of *Wuthering Heights* did on Sunday afternoons with Heathcliff and

9. Ibid., 89.

Catherine. Still, small doses of practice in reading and thinking, when undertaken regularly, will be of lifelong benefit.

How to Know

- Provide books.
- Develop reading skills.
- Make time for reading books.
- Learn to read nonfiction with attentiveness, care, and diligence.
- Learn to summarize, reflect on, and question the truth of non-fiction literature.
- Train the imagination by developing an appreciation for fiction literature.

CONSIDER THE CLASSICAL APPROACH

In recent decades, a number of schools, both Christian and secular, have adopted what is known as the classical model of education. Ancient Rome, having conquered the known world and made slaves of multitudes, had more than enough people to do every workaday task and fill every trade. The result: plenty of leisure time for Roman citizens, for the free people, to learn and to study and to pursue those things that *human beings* (as opposed to other creatures) find interesting—history, literature, language, art, philosophy, music, etc.—those things we call the *humanities*. (These are also known as the "liberal arts"; the free, or "liber," people were the ones who studied them.)

People of ancient times divided these things into three categories, and called the whole the *trivium*. One category was grammar, the basic facts of a subject; another category was dialectic (sometimes called logic), the way to think about a subject, putting together all its different components to make sense of it all; and the third category was rhetoric, the practical use and application of a subject. The most popular model of classical education in our time takes off from an essay by Dorothy Sayers, "The Lost Tools of Learning,"[10] in which she

---

10. This essay can be found in Appendix A of Douglas Wilson's *Recovering the Lost Tools of Learning: An Approach to a Distinctively Christian Education* (Wheaton, IL: Crossway Books, 1991), 145–64.

suggests that childhood itself can be broken down into three stages that match these three categories. Sayers proposes that, since young children so easily memorize and since they love rhythm, chant, and song, teachers should fill their heads full of the grammar of all the different subjects during the preteen years. In math, they should be memorizing and drilling math facts; in their native language, they should memorize spelling and grammar rules; in reading, they should be drilling phonics; in history, names, places, and dates. About the time children are ready for junior high, noted Sayers, an argumentative streak begins to surface. Children this age want to know "why" about everything and they often think in terms of "what if." They have an argument ready on almost any topic, because their brains are learning how to analyze information and options. Children of this age are well suited for the dialectic or logic stage, which involves questioning known facts, learning to put them together so they make sense, and learning to reason logically. In their late teen/early adult years, young people yearn to express themselves, telling what they think and feel and why they think and feel it. That's the age when rhetoric should be taught—the best and clearest way to write and speak in order to use and to apply all they've learned so far.

This model has a lot to commend it for use in educating children in Bible and doctrine. Coauthors Gene Edward Veith and Andrew Kern write, "To be educated in any subject, you must 1) know its basic facts (grammar); 2) be able to reason clearly about it (logic); and 3) apply it personally in an effective way (rhetoric)."[11] Later, they explain, "Each element in the trivium is essential. . . . Factual knowledge (grammar) is useless without understanding (logic). Knowledge and understanding mean little unless they can be expressed and applied (rhetoric)."[12] And of course, first and foremost, there must be an adequate supply of the grammar ("Just the facts, ma'am"). You can neither understand nor apply what you don't know.

11. Gene Edward Veith Jr. and Andrew Kern, *Classical Education: Towards the Revival of American Schooling* (Washington, DC: Capital Research Center, 1997), 12.
12. Ibid., 13.

For the purpose of this book, which stresses providing our children with the head knowledge of Christianity, it's important to consider what is the "grammar" of Bible and Christian doctrine. What is the core foundation of knowledge our children should know by the time they reach middle school? The grammar of Bible would include knowing the books of the Bible and the Ten Commandments. It would include a comprehensive knowledge of important Bible people, Bible places, and Bible events. In addition, children can easily memorize even whole passages of Scripture at this age (and, unlike at later ages, retain it!). Things memorized now—and faithfully drilled—will be remembered for life. (Wouldn't *you* love to know just where Habakkuk comes in your Bible without relying on the contents page?) As for the grammar of Christian doctrine, nothing surpasses a good, biblical catechism for use at this stage—but more on that in chapter 13.

Once again, let me pause to consider the objection that this is only information; where's the application? We do aim for age-appropriate application, but let me remind you, we're trying to think long term. There is no need to feel guilty about emphasizing information. When we teach phonics, we give students practice in using the sounds by putting together words, but we don't feel pressured to apply those phonics immediately by requiring children to read a Shakespeare play. That can come later; for now, we're preparing young readers to be able to appreciate Hamlet when they are older. Likewise, there is value in filling children with knowledge of the Bible and of Christian doctrine now, to prepare them to reason about it and apply it in the future.

Classical educators realize that learning is a lifelong pursuit. The objective, therefore, is to build into children tools for learning that will last them a lifetime. Imagine entering adolescence, with all its demands for life decisions, already possessing a thorough knowledge of God's Word and of sound doctrine as a basis for making those decisions. Imagine going on into adulthood and taking a place of ministry in the church and in the world, having already mastered a wealth of knowledge in the Scriptures and in Christian doctrine.

Wouldn't every Christian parent or teacher want this for children? No one would argue against this goal.

But this won't just happen through hit-or-miss lessons and stories. Wise teachers of any subject, when teaching elementary "grammar stage" children, follow a diligent, systematic plan. One set of math facts builds on the last set learned. A well-thought order and diligence in drilling permeate the whole body of knowledge being taught. Wise Christian parents and teachers will do the same, filling young minds with Christian truth and Bible facts while they still find it easy to learn and memorize. In this way, we equip them with tools that will prove invaluable to them in their subsequent stages of maturity and learning.

How to Know

- Teach elementary-aged (and younger) children important Bible facts and doctrinal concepts.
- Memorize, memorize, memorize, and drill, drill, drill.
- Be patient. Teach lots of content now, and be willing to wait for future application.
- Recognize that Christian education is a lifelong pursuit. Provide tools for learning now that will last your children a lifetime.

KEEP YOUR BALANCE

As I close this chapter of general "how-tos" for teaching Bible and doctrine, I want to leave you with two thoughts intended to balance each other. The first is this: maintain high expectations for children. As I've taught elementary-school-aged children over the years, I've learned that, even though high academic standards can seem tough for my young students, when I lower the standards a little to help them out, suddenly, those new, lower standards seem too hard for them. If the standards are high, some students won't excel, and few will always have perfect papers. But when I lower the standards, the numbers of excelling students and of perfect papers really don't change much. Children will not rise *higher* than our expectations. When we keep our expectations high, they stretch to reach and will actually perform better than when we lower the standards to try to help them.

We live in an age that expects very little of children. Many of today's young adolescents find themselves completely baffled by a book like *Treasure Island*, written, several generations ago, for children younger than they are. No one has expected these modern teens to master the reading and vocabulary skills needed for such a book, or to drill and practice those skills. It has been easier all around to lower the expectations for what children should be able to read. In countless areas, our expectations of children in twenty-first-century America are low. We tend to think that children can't possibly engage in anything that does not constantly change and entertain. They can't possibly enjoy classical music or art masterpieces. They can't possibly sit through a worship service. Everything must be centered on them, and adapted to their interests, and to what they find easy and fun. If we want our children to learn biblical doctrine, we begin by raising our expectations and keeping them high. This will involve swimming against contemporary currents, even in most churches and in most Bible curricula, where keeping it "fun for the kids" has become a top priority. Instead, we will provide an atmosphere in the home, in the Sunday school classroom, and in the worship service that communicates to children our expectation that they will participate, with God's people, in the reading and hearing of God's Word. Children can understand that the Word of God matters to the people who matter to them, and that those people intend for them, the children, to take part in learning what it teaches.

My other closing thought, meant to balance that last one, is this: On the other hand, *do* make concessions for children, *because* they're children. Too often, in religious contexts, when adults have high expectations of children, that's all they have. We need to balance our high expectations with genuine compassion for the nature of a child. *We're* the adults; *we're* the ones to whom doctrine is so important; shouldn't we have to do at least as much work in making that doctrine understandable as the children have to do in meeting our high expectations? With God's Word containing such rich truth, it is inexcusable to give our children only "fluff" or only moral lessons. But it's also wrong to fail to recognize the needs children have when we teach. They need things to be simple. They need words defined. They need illustrations and repetition. They need things to *do* to help keep them engaged. In an address to teachers of children, Charles Spurgeon wrote, "You must next strive to adapt yourself as far as possible to the nature, and habits, and temperament of the child. Your mouth must find out the child's words, so that the child may know what you mean; you must see things with a child's eyes."[13] Any pastor or teacher wants to know how best to communicate to his particular audience. In the same way, as teachers of children—or as pastors preaching to congregations that include children—we need to consider them, to think through their limitations and how we can assist them to understand our teaching. What do they already know that we can springboard from to teach them something new? What words can we use to explain a new term they haven't heard before? Away with the idea that teaching kids is easy, something anyone can do without any effort at all. Spurgeon continues, "It needs our best wits, our most industrious studies, our most earnest thoughts, our ripest powers, to teach our little ones."[14]

And here's an added bonus, given also by Spurgeon. We may not know these things well ourselves. But as we teach them, we will learn them. Or we may know, inside out, the truths we'll be passing on to our children. Even so, we will find our hearts drawn after our God in worship as we focus on these things in order to teach them to children. Spurgeon reminds us:

> There is no way of learning like teaching, and you do not know a thing till you can teach it to another. You do not thoroughly know any truth till you can put it before a child so that he can see it. In

13. Charles Spurgeon, *Come, Ye Children: A Book for Parents and Teachers on the Christian Training of Children* (Pasadena, TX: Pilgrim Publications), 157.
14. Ibid.

trying to make a little child understand the doctrine of the atonement you will get clearer views of it yourselves, and therefore I commend the holy exercise to you.[15]

How to Know

- Maintain high expectations.
- Make concessions for children because they are children—keep things simple, define words, illustrate, and repeat.
- Keep balanced.

15. Ibid., 73.

12

The "Grammar" of Bible: Foundations of Teaching Bible to Children

If the grammar of a subject is its memorizable facts and rules, the basic skeleton that underlies all the rest of the subject matter, what would the grammar of the Bible be? It would include key verses or passages to memorize, such as the Ten Commandments, the Lord's Prayer, the Beatitudes, some psalms, and some important passages on salvation. Matthew Henry wrote, "Though the words alone without the things will do us no good, yet we are in danger of losing the things if we neglect the words, by which ordinarily divine light and power are conveyed to the heart."[1] Bible grammar would involve knowing the books of the Bible in order, with their divisions (law; history; poetry or wisdom books; prophets, both major and minor; gospels; epistles). The grammar of the Bible would include its main characters, its main events, its main place names, and a basic idea of what order these things come in.

The most logical way to teach Bible characters, events, and places is through telling Bible stories. Children love stories, and those of us who teach them are thankful God included so many in his Word. In fact, God has ordained stories as one of the primary ways he communicates the truth about who he is and about his relationship with his people. This brings up an important consideration as we prepare to teach our children: there is a right way and there are wrong ways to tell Bible stories.

1. Matthew Henry, *Commentary on the Whole Bible Volume 1* (Grand Rapids: Christian Classics Ethereal Library), http://www.ccel.org/ccel/henry/mhc1.i.html.

GETTING TO THE POINT OF THE STORIES WE TELL

Consider what the Bible is. Is it inspiration for daily life? Is it moral instruction? Is it comfort and encouragement for facing the difficulties of each day? Is it a collection of examples of how to live life at its fullest? Certainly, the Bible provides these things, and this is what many people who read the Bible look for when they read it. To look only for inspiration, moral instruction, encouragement, and examples, however, is to come at the Bible with a me-centered approach. What can the Bible do for *me*? None of these things defines what the Bible is first and foremost.

In the Bible, we find the record of what God has done, specifically in providing redemption for his people. From the beginning, it was God's plan to have a people for himself, and to be the God of those people. Beginning in the Bible's very first chapters, we see this purpose, seemingly thwarted early on (the fall), attacked and opposed over and over, but marching onward without fail through every story. *The Bible, therefore, including its stories, is the record of the redemption God provides and the revelation of his character.*

Our most common practices with the Bible often fail to reckon with Scripture as the revelation of God's character and the record of God's salvation. We read little snippets, isolated from their contexts, for wisdom for this day as though we're sampling fortune cookies. We spend all our time in our favorite books and passages. Our Bible studies revolve around answering, "What does this passage say to you?" When we teach Bible stories to our children, we draw moral applications at the end from what the characters did. But, often, we fail to consider: what does this passage show me about who God is and what God has done?

When we teach a Bible story to children, we want to present it in such a way that God's reason for including this particular story shines through. We want to show how this narrative fits into the overarching, main story of God accomplishing redemption so he could have a people for his own possession. As we present the Bible stories like this, our emphasis is on what God has done and each story of his mighty acts reveals another aspect of his great character.

The most common misuse of Bible stories with children presents the stories as examples of good and bad behavior or good and bad character. When taught like this, Bible stories focus on the human characters, holding them up as people the children should (and, in some cases, should not) imitate. Be brave like David, and you'll be able to overcome the giants in your life. When you hear of Cain and Abel or Jacob and Esau, resolve not to quarrel with your siblings, as they did. Let the story of Joseph and his brothers remind you that you, too, can forgive those who wrong you. Be unselfish like Abraham, who let Lot choose the best land for himself. The problem with this, though, is that God did not intend the stories to be showcases of moral glory for human beings; he intended them to reveal himself to his people.

The other misuse of Bible stories with children makes the child and his concerns central. God is portrayed as someone the child can count on to relieve all his distresses and give him what he needs (wants?). Jesus calmed a storm. If you ask him, he will protect you from whatever you fear. God gave manna in the wilderness. God will take care of you and your physical needs as well. The baby Moses' mother hid him and his sister watched over him; God gives us families to take care of us. When Jesus prayed, God led him to the right choices for disciples; God will give us friends if we ask him. There are (at least) two problems with this approach. The first is that there are plenty of children in this world who *aren't* protected from what they fear, who *don't* have enough to eat, whose families hurt them, or who have no friends. How do we tell them these stories? The other problem is that this approach makes a servant of God, someone to come running when we whistle, a genie we can call on when something isn't the way we'd like it to be.

Instead of a moralistic approach or a child-centered approach when we teach the Bible's stories, we want to present Bible stories from a God-centered approach. What is *God* doing in this story? How do his actions in this story show us what he's like? I once heard an illustration in which the Bible was likened to a museum whose subject is God. Each passage of Scripture was compared to a different exhibit in the museum, each providing a different angle or highlighting another facet of the richness of God's character. Every story in the Bible is one of these exhibits, calling us to marvel at yet one more wonderful thing about our God.[2] This is how we need to tell the Bible stories to our children, refusing to allow ourselves to be sidetracked by anything less.

Let's consider two stories, one from the Old Testament and one from the New, to see how the three approaches—moralistic, child-centered, and God-centered—differ.

1 Kings 17:8–16 tells the story of Elijah going, at God's command, to stay with a poor widow and her son during a three-year drought in Israel. Food was running scarce for everyone and, when Elijah first met this widow, she was gathering wood to make a fire. He asked her if she would give him a drink of water and a morsel of bread. The widow told Elijah that she had just enough flour and oil to make one last cake for her son and herself, so that, she said, "We may eat it and die." Elijah told her to make a cake *first* for him, and then for her son and herself. God had promised, he assured her, that her jar of flour and her jug of oil would not be empty until God sent rain to end the drought. The widow believed what Elijah told her and made his bread first. Sure enough, "she and her household ate for many days," and the flour and oil didn't run out until the rains came again.

The moralistic approach to this story encourages the children to be like the widow and to give to God's work, or to share with others, before they spend what they have on their own wants and needs. When they do this, God will surely give them enough for themselves as well. The child-centered approach assures children that God knows what they need and will provide for them. While both of these may be good points that have their place, neither is the main point of this story. They are not the reason God had this story included in Scripture.

The book of Kings, where we find this story, begins with Solomon ruling the united kingdom of Israel. Once he dies and the kingdom divides into a northern kingdom of Israel and a southern kingdom of Judah, the focus of the book moves back and forth from one kingdom to the other, tracing the fidelity (occasionally) and the

2. I am indebted to Ray Ortlund, Jr. for this illustration.

infidelity (usually) of the rulers of God's people. It was during the rule of these kings that the prophets wrote or, like Elijah, spoke. One of the most important messages the prophets brought was that God alone is God. Whatever he speaks comes to pass. Always. The prophets were ever speaking against Israel's ongoing love affair with other gods, who could do nothing. The context of this particular story is the rule of wicked King Ahab over Israel, influenced by his Baal-worshiping foreign wife to eradicate the worship of God and to promote the worship of Baal. Since Baal was considered the storm god, he should be able to make it rain. God said, through Elijah, that there would be no rain, and there hadn't been. That was how the famine had begun. At first, God told Elijah he had "commanded" the ravens to provide Elijah's food. Then God sent him to a widow whom he had "commanded" to feed him. When the widow told Elijah that she didn't have enough food for him, his answer was, "Thus says the LORD, the God of Israel, 'The jar of flour shall not be spent, and the jug of oil shall not be empty, until the day that the LORD sends rain upon the earth'" (1 Kings 17:14). God's people needed to see that God's word always comes to pass, because he is God. The passage ends by saying that all this happened "according to the word of the LORD he spoke by Elijah" (v. 16). *There* is the point. God is God; all that he says will always come to pass. To rely on any other god is sheer foolishness because this one rules just by speaking.

Acts 12 tells the story, humorous in parts, of Peter's escape from Herod's jail. Herod had imprisoned both James and Peter and had executed James. When he saw how well that pleased the Jews, Herod planned to execute Peter as well. The night before the execution was scheduled, an angel entered Peter's cell, woke him, caused his chains to fall off, and led him through gates that opened of their own accord, past sleeping guards who never woke. It took Peter some time to realize he wasn't dreaming. Once he understood that he was, in fact, free, he went to the home where Christians had gathered to pray for him. They also had a hard time believing he was free and, for a while, they insisted that the servant girl, who had announced that Peter was knocking at the gate, must be wrong. Peter had to knock for some time before his friends finally believed it *was* Peter and let him in.

The morals-focused or need-focused teachers would probably stop the story here. The moralistic teacher would tell the children that they should pray, as the Christians had done for Peter, and that they should believe God can answer their prayers, as those Christians, for a while, failed to do. The need-focused (child-centered) teacher would make the point that children don't need to be afraid because God will always protect them (though this teacher may want to hurry past the part of the story where James had already been executed).

The God-centered teacher, though, considers the book of Acts as a whole and goes on to the end of this particular chapter. The book of Acts outlines the progress of the gospel from Jerusalem through "all Judea and Samaria, and to the end of the earth" (Acts 1:8), in spite of an onslaught of opposition from many sources. It demonstrates all that Jesus continued "to do and teach" (v. 1) even after "he was taken up" (v. 2). He sends out his Word in power and none can stop it. In this particular story, King Herod tried to stop the gospel's advance by intending to put to death two of its main spokesmen, but God overruled him. Not only was Herod unable to kill and silence Peter as he intended, but he also suffered a gruesome, inglorious death at the end of the story. After Herod had received the praise of his subjects for being a god, an angel of the Lord struck him "because he did not give God the glory, and he was eaten by worms and breathed his last. But," Luke adds, in contrast, "the word of God increased and multiplied" (Acts 12:22–24). God accomplishes his purposes, regardless of who stands in the way. He uses the gospel in power, regardless of who opposes it and how they oppose it. God had sent his long-promised Messiah, redemption had been accomplished, he was sending the message about it to the ends of the earth, and it could not be stopped. *There's* the point of the story. It's found in what God does in the story and what we learn from it of his character.

It's easy to feel we must make a moral lesson of the story or show the child how it applies to a concern he or she has this very day.

After all, we want Scripture to be relevant to the children, practical for right now. But we must be willing to think more long-term. We need to think less in terms of action points to apply in the next day or two, and think more in terms of "belief points"[3] that affect a child's long-term way of thinking and will come to influence all his behavior, all the time.

In order to read and tell Bible stories so that we're making the author's and God's point, rather than our own, it's imperative to know the author's intention for the book where we found the story. Sometimes the author tells us that clearly, as Luke does in the beginning of his gospel and in the beginning of Acts, or as John does at the end of his gospel (John 20:30–31). Sometimes we find the author's intention as we study the book, noting recurring phrases as in the book of Judges.[4] Sometimes we may need the help of those who have studied much longer and more in-depth than we have, so we can turn to a book's introduction in a trusted study Bible or in a commentary.

An overall picture of the whole of redemption history and where this particular book fits will also aid in getting at a particular story's purpose. Is this more work than just reading the story and coming up with an on-the-surface point that may not be God's point? Of course it is. But it gets at what God wanted us to know by giving us that story. It helps us see who God is and what he will be for his people. So it is infinitely worth the trouble.

How to Know

- Learn to see the Bible as the revelation of the character of God and of the redemption he provides.
- Resist focusing primarily on human characters when you teach Bible stories to children.

---

3. John H. Walton and Kim E. Walton, *The Bible Story Handbook: A Resource for Teaching 175 Stories from the Bible* (Wheaton, IL: Crossway, 2010), 18.

4. The repeated sentence "In those days there was no king in Israel" and the longer "In those days there was no king in Israel. Everyone did what was right in his own eyes" (Judg. 18:1, 19:1, 17:6, 21:25) give the reader a hint that the author wrote to show the need for a godly leader of God's people.

- Help children see what God is doing in the Bible story and what that shows us about what he is like.
- Resist both moralistic and child-centered approaches to Bible stories; make your teaching God-centered.
- Rather than demanding "action points" in your teaching that children can apply right now, keep "belief points" in mind that will serve your children for a lifetime.
- To get at the main point of the Bible story, learn the author's intention for the book the story is in.

A BRIEF SURVEY OF HOW REDEMPTION HISTORY SHOWS US GOD

To be sure you're reading—and telling—Bible narrative from a God-centered perspective, you can ask yourself two questions at the end of each story you encounter. First, where does this story fit in the overall account of redemption history? Secondly, what do we learn about God from this story?

Redemption history begins in the book of beginnings, Genesis, where God creates a perfect world for his people, who almost immediately devastate it by choosing sin. In the creation story, we learn all this about God: he is eternal and self-existent; he is sovereign; he speaks and his word is powerful; he is infinitely wise and infinitely good. In the story of the fall, we see God's holiness, judgment, grace, faithfulness, perseverance in his good purpose, and commitment to long-term war and final victory over sin and Satan. In Genesis, we also have the beginning of the people of God in the stories of Abraham and his family. We see God initiating a covenant that will last forever. We see that he intends to include people from all the nations in that covenant, and we learn that faith is the basis for his counting his people righteous when they really are quite sinful. When God repeatedly acts on behalf of deceitful Jacob, we understand God to be a God of grace, and when he preserves the family through Joseph's rise from slavery to leadership in Egypt, we see God's wisdom, sovereignty, and faithfulness even in difficult providences.

In the stories of Exodus, Leviticus, and Numbers, we see that God raises up a redeemer for his people, a picture of the greater Redeemer he will bring in Christ. We marvel at the fact that God is a God who tells us his name, who reveals himself to us, because he wants a relationship with us. We see his power over all creation in the plagues and as he provides for his people in the wilderness. We tremble with the Israelites when he gives his law, so perfect we will never keep it, but we sigh with relief at his provision of sacrifices for atonement. In the instructions for the tabernacle, the priesthood, and the sacrifices, we learn that God dictates the terms on which people can come to him; they cannot simply barge into his presence any old way, but must come through the means he has provided. This is a truth we will apply when we encounter Jesus in the New Testament and hear him say that *he* is "the way" and no one comes to the Father but through him (John 14:6).

As the Israelites wander in the wilderness, we wonder at the longsuffering of God, who continues faithful in spite of all the Israelites do that would discourage faithfulness. In Joshua, we see God keep his promises to give the people the land and, in Judges, we see how patiently God continues to bear with them, though he has to send discipline against them time and time again. We watch the unlikely heroes he raises up to deliver them when they cry to him, and we learn that God delights in using the weak, the small, the unlikely, so that all the glory will go to him alone. We learn from Judges how desperately God's people need a godly king, and we watch him begin to provide it in the book of Ruth, even as he also converts a pagan woman and preserves a godly Israelite in the midst of general ungodliness.

Samuel introduces us to prophets and kings. We meet David, the king after God's own heart. God raises him up, uses him, preserves him through conflict, and blesses his people through his godly reign—as he will do for his descendant, God promises. God also forgives David, which he will *not* have to do with the perfect descendant to come. The books of the Kings give us the explanation for why God's people did not remain in the land. God was faithful to his threats of judgment as well as to his promises for good. God's people rejected him and his covenant and would not repent, in spite of all his patience and in spite of all the warnings he sent via the prophets; therefore, God sent judgment and they went into exile.

We have stories of God's people in exile, most notably in the book of Daniel. Though it appeared that God's relationship with his people had ended—the land emptied, the temple destroyed, the people scattered, and their enemies triumphant—Daniel shows us God as the Most High, in every story in the book as well as in the visions Daniel has. We have the promise in Daniel that God's kingdom will come and will be the only one to endure; he *will* have that people for himself, to rule with him forever, as he purposed all along. In Ezra, Nehemiah, and Esther we have stories again of God's faithfulness to keep his promises and to keep his people, as the Jews return and rebuild and as Esther, through a series of "coincidences," keeps the nation from being exterminated.

Then Jesus bursts onto the scene in the Gospels and begins to fulfill every Old Testament promise, showing himself to be the substance that so many things in the Old Testament foreshadowed. His miracles make clear his divinity. His teaching is with authority as being from God himself. He suffers and dies, then rises from the dead and explains to the followers he had taught for three years that every part of the Scriptures speak of him. Before returning to the Father, Jesus sends his apostles out into all the world to tell of his life and death, to explain what it meant, and to proclaim forgiveness of sins in his name. The book of Acts, the last book of the Bible to tell stories of people and events, describes the victorious spread of the gospel of Jesus Christ and the growth of his church.

How to Know

- Get to know the *whole* Bible, and teach children the *whole* Bible.

A GUIDE TO FINDING A BIBLE STORY'S MEANING

If you can answer these questions about the Bible narrative you are reading or teaching, you probably understand why God had it included right here in this particular book of the Bible.

1. How does the book that contains this story fit in the overall Bible story?
2. Where does this story fit in the overall story of its book?
3. What was the author's purpose for writing the book? What did he want his original audience to know or understand?
4. How does this particular story further the author's overall purpose for this book?
5. What would the author have wanted his original audience to believe and/or do as a result of reading this story?
6. What general principles, true in all times and all places, can we deduce from that?
7. How should that general principle make a difference to us?

Most people want to read the story in isolation from any other passage, then go directly to the seventh question on the list. You may be thinking that working through a list such as this is a lot of work, and you're right; it is. But it's work that has rich return, because it results in a clearer understanding of, and therefore a deeper love for, our great God. It helps us see what God wanted us to see about himself when he included this particular story, and what could be better than that? God has chosen to reveal himself in a book, and a book, to be rightly understood, must be known in its entirety. You would not expect to read a paragraph from the middle of *Moby Dick* or a page from Edward Gibbons's *Fall and Decline of the Roman Empire* and think you had grasped what the author wanted you to know. With the Bible, too, it isn't just seminary students who should study it, but any who want to know and love their God.

How to Know
- Ask yourself the questions from the list above to get at the meaning of a Bible story.

AD FONTES—BACK TO THE SOURCE!
One component of classical education and a factor in kicking off the Reformation is the idea that the best way to study something is to go

to the original text. In the fifteenth century, a movement in education set students to learning classical languages so they could study original sources in classical literature. When people studied the original Greek of the New Testament, they saw that much of what they had been taught by the church of the day was not biblical at all, and the Reformation exploded. While most of us will not be teaching our children Greek and Hebrew so they can study Scripture in its original languages, we should at least be helping our children use the original source of the doctrine we teach them, and that is the Bible itself.

From its earliest days, the church has faced teachers of false doctrine and preachers of "another gospel" (see Gal. 1:8). That's why New Testament writers always called believers to hold to the teaching they had received from Christ and from his apostles. There is a standard. Any teaching claiming to be from God must always be compared to the standard. We teach our children what the Bible says, and we want them to believe that what it says is true. As they grow, however, they'll come into contact with *unfaithful* teachers, who either deliberately undermine biblical doctrine or who don't know it well enough to present it accurately. How will our children know when they hear *unsound* doctrine? We do them a great service if we teach them how to use their Bibles and if we develop in them habits of listening to new ideas with their Bibles open.

To that end, we need to be sure children have Bibles and know their way around in them. Just as with riding a bicycle or solving math problems, using the Bible is a skill that must be *practiced*. Teachers and parents must make opportunities for children to not just *hear* what the Bible says but to practice using the Bible for themselves.

One of the most basic places to begin is by teaching children the names of the Bible's books, in order, and then reviewing them periodically, so they don't forget them. Then we need to teach them how to find things in their Bibles and provide them with opportunities for practice. It often comes as a surprise to parents to realize that their school-age children do not know how to look up a Bible verse. Looking up something in the Bible is more complicated than simply turning to page 34 in some other book. Children need to know that the first number in a Bible reference refers to a chapter, and the second number refers to a verse. Then they need to know how to find chapter numbers and verse numbers on the pages of their own Bibles, and they need to have some idea of where in the Bible to find the particular book they're looking for.

At home and in church classes or Christian school classes, give children plenty of practice in using their Bibles. Many Sunday school teachers think they've done their job if they've accurately explained to children what the Bible says. In this case, though, the *method* matters, as well as the message. If children only *listen* to a teacher or parent tell about the Bible, and don't actually *see* what it says, they learn to depend on people in authority to tell them what the Bible teaches. This sets them up to be misled by someone who seems to know but who falsely represents the Bible's teaching. We need to train children to read and study *the Bible*, not to simply take someone else's word about what it contains.

With children too young to read, show them where in a real Bible (not just in a Bible storybook) this particular story or verse is found. With children who are just beginning to read, let them find, in the Bible passage, the name of the main human character in the story. Or let them sound out a short, key verse in the lesson, making sure they do this from their Bibles, and not from a Sunday school handout.

Teach children who can read to find things in the text. Ask them "who-what-when-where-why" questions about a passage, and let them find the answers. Ask them questions about the text they read, having them look for specific things in the passage itself. Don't accept an answer, even if it's correct, *unless* they found it in the verse itself. For instance, if you are looking together at Jesus' words in John 6:38 ("For I have come down from heaven, not to do my own will but the will of him who sent me"), and if you ask, "According to this verse, why did Jesus come to earth?" your child may answer, "To die for our sins." It's the easy answer; they already knew it. "That's true," you would say, "but there was a big reason behind that. What does it say in *this* verse?" Train them to read carefully and to see what the text of Scripture actually says.

You can also train children to read with specific themes in mind. As you read through Bible passages, they could highlight specific themes in particular colors: God's covenant with his people, for example, or Christ the Savior.[5] This will help them to understand that the Bible is not a collection of random writings or wise or moralistic sayings, but one book with central themes that carry through the whole thing. It will help them learn to read with the big picture of God's revelation in mind.

Sunday school teachers can encourage their young students to use their Bibles by providing ample opportunity to use them in class, especially with children old enough to be competent readers. Teachers can provide other passages that relate to the day's lesson that children can look up. In this way, the children will not only see that the Bible is a unified whole but they will also gain practice in using it. Or teachers can show children how to use the cross-references in their own Bibles to find additional verses. Many Sunday school curricula provide a student worksheet for each lesson that has the day's Bible passage printed on it. Relying on these worksheets will not help your students learn to use their Bibles. Require children to bring Bibles; then make sure they will need them. Here I will admit that I have never hesitated to sink to bribery. I have a box of mini candy bars in my Sunday school classroom—the kinds of candy children actually like, not simply nondescript hard candies—and my students know that anyone who brings a Bible may choose from the box at the end of class. I have had 100 percent participation in Bible-toting for years! (And many Bibles are inexpensive, so no church will balk at giving a Bible to a child who doesn't have one anywhere in his home.)

Do whatever you can to give children opportunities to use their Bibles. Take them back to the source of the doctrine you teach them. Train them to use God's Word. In this way, you'll communicate to them that God's people treasure God's book—not only in word, but also in deed and in truth.

One aspect of the grammar of Christian truth is basic Bible knowledge, but key doctrinal truth is another. If we teach Bible stories separated from Bible doctrine, Abraham, Moses, and Paul join the ranks of our other literary friends—Robin Hood or Cinderella or Charlotte

---

5. I am indebted to Susan Hunt for this idea.

(the one with the web). They become heroes to imitate, rather than recipients of God's gracious covenant promises, who came to know and understand and love and trust God. If our teaching is mostly moral in nature, we teach a works-righteousness that runs counter to the gospel. The deliberate, systematic instruction of our children in sound biblical doctrine gives an accurate, defining framework for the Bible stories we tell and the morals we want them to hold. Therefore, we must teach doctrine, too, if the stories are to carry the meaning God intended for them to have when he included them in Scripture. It is to this aspect of Christian grammar that we turn next.

How to Know

- Provide children with their own Bibles.
- At home and in Bible or Sunday school classes, use Bibles regularly.
- Have children memorize the books of the Bible in order.
- Show young children where in a real Bible we find the story you are about to read.
- Let beginning readers sound out a name or an important word from the story as it is found in the Bible.
- Teach children who can read how to find things in their Bibles.
- Teach children to ask questions to see what is actually in the text in front of them.
- Teach children to look for and highlight recurring themes in the whole Bible.

13

The "Grammar" of Doctrine: Have You Considered a Catechism?

DOCTRINE? FOR KIDS?

"I do hold that there is no doctrine of the Word of God which a child, if he be capable of salvation, is not capable of receiving. I would have children taught all the great doctrines of truth without a solitary exception that they may in their after days hold fast by them."[1] So wrote Charles Spurgeon in a book of addresses intended for teachers of children. Likewise, nineteenth-century theologian, Charles Hodge, wrote, "Every doctrine which can be taught to theologians is taught to children. . . . The important truth is that there are not two sets of doctrine, a higher and a lower form of faith, one for the learned and the other for the unlearned; there is no part of the gospel which we are authorized to keep back from the people."[2]

Doctrine is not the first thing we think of when we think of what to teach children. And the younger the child, the more this is the case. Doctrine is theology. It's philosophical. It's abstract. Everyone knows children cannot grasp abstract concepts before a certain point in their development. And what concepts these are! Many of the theological truths we know boggle *our* minds. How would we ever explain them to children? But when we stop and consider the infinitely great God, we must realize—that's just the

1. Charles Spurgeon, *Come, Ye Children: A Book for Parents and Teachers on the Christian Training of Children* (Pasadena, TX: Pilgrim Publications, 1975), 99.
2. Charles Hodge, *Commentary on First Corinthians* (Titus Books, 2013), chap. 3, Kindle.

point. What *is* the age when a finite human being can clearly grasp all there is to know about God? If they live to be two hundred, our children will never be so intellectually mature that the truths God has revealed about himself will make perfect sense to them. When it comes to understanding the infinite, inscrutable *God*, the most brilliant mind ever created is in the bottom level of nursery school. God, in his grace, reveals truth to minds of whatever age, when his people faithfully proclaim his word. As Jesus prayed, "I thank you, Father, Lord of heaven and earth, that you have hidden these things from the wise and understanding and revealed them to little children; yes, Father, for such was your gracious will" (Luke 10:21). God calls us to teach all of his truth to all of his people. We do so in the confidence that he himself will impart the understanding an individual needs at his or her particular place of spiritual growth. We teach doctrine *as* our children grow up, rather than *after* they have grown up, because failure to teach sound doctrine results in children learning unsound doctrine.

J. I. Packer bemoans the loss of doctrinal instruction in families and churches. In particular, he writes that the church used to rely on catechesis for such instruction and has come to neglect it to its great loss. He defines catechesis, in part, as "intentional, orderly instruction in the truths that Christians are called to live by," and writes that its "intended end product is Christians who know their faith, can explain it to enquirers and sustain it against skeptics, and can put it to work in evangelism, church fellowship, and the many forms of service to God and man for which circumstances call."[3]

How to Know

- Make doctrinal instruction a part of teaching children.
- Children are never too young to start learning Bible doctrine.

CATECHISM? FOR PROTESTANTS? WHAT ABOUT THE BIBLE?

As the name suggests, catechesis involves making use of a catechism, a question-and-answer guide for teaching important truths. When

3. J. I. Packer, *Taking God Seriously: Vital Things We Need to Know* (Wheaton, IL: Crossway, 2013), 10–11.

186

most evangelical Christians first hear someone suggest that they use a catechism to teach, they think, "But catechisms are for Catholics!" This is probably because Roman Catholics continued the use of catechisms after most Protestant churches dropped them so that, in more recent times, we find mostly Catholics using them. A glance back into history, however, would change our perspective. Formal statements of the faith have circulated from the earliest days of the Christian church. These creedal statements would extract, from the totality of the Scriptures, the essence of key truths, and state them in simple, concise form. This made it possible to examine candidates for baptism, making sure they believed these essential Christian doctrines. But it was the Protestant Reformers who wrote catechisms. When the Catholic Church saw how effective Reformers were in teaching the Protestant faith, the Catholic Counter-Reformation wrote its own new catechism as well.

Martin Luther explained why he wrote a catechism. He wrote of his dismay at the ignorance of basic biblical truth displayed by professing Christians. He pleaded with pastors to use the catechism he had written to help fill up what was lacking. "The deplorable, miserable condition which I discovered lately when I, too, was a visitor, has forced and urged me to prepare [publish] this Catechism, or Christian doctrine, in this small, plain, simple form. . . . What manifold misery I beheld! The common people, especially in the villages, have no knowledge whatever of Christian doctrine, and, alas! many pastors are altogether incapable and incompetent to teach. Nevertheless, all maintain that they are Christians, have been baptized and receive the holy Sacraments. Yet they do not understand and cannot even recite either the Lord's Prayer, or the Creed, or the Ten Commandments." He begged pastors "to have pity on the people who are entrusted to you, and to help us inculcate the Catechism upon the people, and especially upon the young."[4] The church in Geneva, under John Calvin, used a catechism. The greatest and best-known Protestant catechisms, the Westminster and the Heidelberg, were written by Reformed teachers

4. Michael Horton, "Conversations for a Modern Reformation," *Modern Reformation*, September/October 2012, 30–31.

and ministers. The idea many of us have about catechisms being for Roman Catholics is a misconception.

The second concern about using a catechism that evangelicals express is, "But a catechism is man-made. Why don't we just have people study the Bible? If they're going to memorize something, why don't they memorize Scripture?" My answer to that is why don't we give them the best of both worlds? Why not have them memorize *both*?

The Bible is the source of all Christian doctrine, and a good catechism teaches only what can be clearly found in Scripture. Most of the doctrine in Scripture, however, is woven into teaching on how to live and love in the church or is illustrated in a story of God's dealings with his people or is found within the lines of a psalmist's prayer of distress. The Bible teaches all the doctrines essential to the Christian faith, but sometimes without stating them in so many words. For example: could you quote a single verse (or even a combination of two or three different ones) clearly stating the doctrine of the Trinity? To find that doctrine in Scripture, you would need to compare multiple passages from all over the Bible. None would spell out a clear statement of Christian belief about the Trinity in so many words. The Westminster Shorter Catechism, though, states it in three short, simple statements, easy to understand and memorize.

Q. 5. Is there more than one God?
A. There is only one, the true and living God.

Q. 6. How many persons are in the one God?
A. Three persons are in the one God, the Father, the Son, and the Holy Spirit. These three are one God, the same in substance and equal in power and glory.[5]

You won't find a statement of the Trinity like this one in the Bible. You'll find the *doctrine* of the Trinity there, but only after you've pulled

5. Douglas Kelly and Philip Rollinson, *The Westminster Shorter Catechism in Modern English* (Phillipsburg, NJ: Presbyterian and Reformed Publishing Company, 1986), 5–6.

together many different passages, examined how those passages relate to each other, and then stated your conclusions in a sentence or two. A catechism gives you that sentence or two. And to try to memorize the doctrine of the Trinity from the Bible would involve memorizing a wide range of Bible texts scattered throughout the Old and New Testaments.

The writers of the best Protestant catechisms were godly men, well-studied in the Scriptures (much more so than most of us!). To use a catechism is to profit from their Spirit-given gifts and from their labors, just as we profit from the labor of our pastors on Sunday morning. Most of us don't really use only the Bible to teach our children. We send them to Sunday school, too, and perhaps to a midweek program as well; we read to them from Bible storybooks. If we really refused to use anything but Scripture, we would be despising the spiritual gifts the Holy Spirit has graciously provided for building up his church.

How to Know

- Use a good, biblically faithful catechism.
- Commit to regular catechetical review.
- Look up and read key Bible texts that are the sources of catechism answers.

WHY CATECHISM? AS A ROAD MAP FOR BIBLE STUDY

Parents and other Bible teachers want children to become well acquainted with God's Word. Becoming well acquainted with a catechism as well will not detract from knowing the Bible; rather, it will enhance Bible study. G. I. Williamson compares a faithful catechism to a map. The map isn't a substitute for physically exploring a geographical area, but it makes our exploration much more productive. Williamson writes:

> We could ask, "Why bother to study a map? Why not just go out and study the surface of the earth instead?" The answer, of course, is that one is wise to begin with a study of maps. After all, life is short and the world is very big. One person, working by himself, could

only map a small portion of the earth's surface. That is why maps are so valuable. They exist because many people over many years have made a study of the earth. And while these maps are not perfect, they are quite accurate. Thus, the best way to begin to understand the geography of the world is not to start with the world itself. No, the best way is to start with a good atlas. Then, after getting hold of the basics one can go out and test the atlas by actually visiting some of the places described in it.

It is much the same with the Bible. The Bible contains a great wealth of information. It isn't easy to master it all—in fact, no one has ever mastered it completely. It would therefore be foolish for us to try to do it on our own, starting from scratch. We would be ignoring all the study of the Word of God that other people have done down through the centuries. That is exactly why we have creeds. They are the product of many centuries of Bible study by a great company of believers. They are a kind of spiritual "road map" of the teaching of the Bible, already worked out and proved by others before us.[6]

A catechism is never meant to replace the Bible. Rather, good catechisms direct our attention to the Bible and bring together its truths. A catechism charts the main features and outlines the grand themes of the Bible, leading us to an orderly understanding, so our reading and our Bible study can become more profitable.

How to Know

- Use a catechism to enhance your study of the Bible.

WHY CATECHISM? AS A MEANS OF GUARDING PRIORITIES

A catechism is the most efficient way to provide careful, systematic instruction in the key doctrines of the Christian faith. It prevents a haphazard, hit-or-miss methodology in teaching. To work through a catechism is to cover every important doctrine, in a relatively short

6. Quoted by Donald Van Dyken in *Rediscovering Catechism: The Art of Equipping Covenant Children* (Phillipsburg, NJ: P&R Publishing, 2000), 22–23.

time, that the Bible teaches, and in a way where the last truth learned builds on the truth taught before that, and supplies the foundation for the truth being taught now. Much religious thought in our culture, and even, sadly, in many of our evangelical churches, is fuzzy and relativistic. Truth, for any given person, has come to mean whatever that person wants to believe is true. Our churches and the people in them may use common God-words, but what those words mean is up for grabs. Each person is free to fill in his or her own definition. Catechisms provide an antidote for such thinking in their cut-and-dried, clear substance, drawn from the Word of God.

In Paul's letter to his "pastoral intern," Timothy, he defines the church as "a pillar and buttress of the truth" (1 Tim. 3:15). One of our primary tasks as a church is to *be* that pillar and buttress, to make sure that we regularly declare and insist upon the truth God has revealed, to make sure we continue to "contend for the faith that was once for all delivered to the saints" (Jude 3). Church and parents will find a catechism enormously helpful in faithfully passing on God's truth to the next generation so that they may contend for it in their day. I paused in the writing of this chapter and went to the website for one of the most commonly used Vacation Bible School curricula available. Its cowboy-themed material promised a "rip-roarin' time with Jesus." Okay, but what will our children *learn* through this curriculum? I searched the web page in vain. I found teachers' books, student books, take-home papers, craft books, skit scripts, puppets, prizes, CDs, and T-shirts; but what would the children *learn*? I saw that I could watch an overview DVD. Surely that would explain what the children would learn, but all the advertisement for it promised was that I would see live-action clips of children "having fun singing, playing games, making crafts, and more." I'm not saying the curriculum *wouldn't* teach the Bible; yet nowhere in the pictures and blurbs advertising what the curriculum contained could I find what that teaching might be. That, evidently, is not a priority. No doubt those who market this curriculum know what churches want. They present, up-front and in full color, what they think churches will look for first. Churches and publishers alike have lost sight of the church's priorities. It's not that it's wrong to use skits and games and crafts and fun themes to teach children; it's that the substance taught by those things should be the *easiest* thing to find in the advertising. It's the *first* thing churches should want to know about a curriculum, not something a potential buyer has to search for and still can't find. The use of faithful catechisms can help the church get its priorities straightened out. Simply, clearly, concisely, they present the truth our children need to know.

How to Know

- Maintain the New Testament focus on teaching doctrinal truth as the church's first priority.
- A catechism can function as a checklist to help you remember what you've covered and what you should review.

WHY CATECHISM? AS A GLOSSARY OF BIBLE TERMS

A good catechism provides an excellent dictionary of terms used in the Bible's own presentation of the gospel. For example, probably the clearest gospel explanation the Bible gives is found in Paul's epistle to the Romans. The core of that explanation is found in Romans 3:21–28. This passage contains some terms that need to be understood before the passage will make sense. Paul presents *sin* as the great human problem, so, to understand the biblical gospel, children need a biblical definition of sin. The Westminster Shorter Catechism provides an excellent, concise definition: "Sin is disobeying or not conforming to God's law in any way."[7] The questions and answers surrounding this definition explain where sin came from, how it entered the world, how it was passed on, the consequences it brings, and God's reaction to it. In short, simple form, the catechism makes clear what sin is and why it's a problem. Our children need this! Too many presentations of the gospel and of Jesus present him as a friend for the lonely, a comfort for the sad, strength for those who struggle, the solution for problems. The Bible presents

7. Kelly and Rollinson, *The Westminster Shorter Catechism*, 7.

him as a Savior for sinners. If we don't receive Jesus as a Savior for sinners, we have not received him as God gave him, and so we have not received the gospel.

This same core passage in Romans 3 tells us that believers are "justified by his grace as a gift." *Justification* is another of the Bible's "technical terms," and one of the most important concepts in the biblical gospel. Can your children explain to you what justification is? Can you explain it? As adults, sure, we know what the term means; we just may not be sure how to explain it. But it's not that difficult. Question 33, again in the Westminster Shorter Catechism, defines it like this: "Justification is the act of God's free grace by which he pardons all our sins and accepts us as righteous in his sight. He does so only because he counts the righteousness of Christ as ours. Justification is received by faith alone."[8] There is no need to wait for seminary to learn that definition. It is short, concise, to the point, easily understandable—and basic to Christianity. Romans 3 also mentions *faith* several times, or "faith in Jesus." The same catechism answers "What is faith in Jesus Christ?" with "Faith in Jesus Christ is a saving grace, by which we receive and rest on him alone for salvation, as he is offered to us in the gospel."[9] There are series of questions in the catechisms, each building on the one before, that define the nature of God, explain the process of redemption, and describe the nature and work of Christ. All are concepts our children—and Christians of any age—need to understand in order to rightly grasp the biblical gospel.

Naturally, we won't be content with our children just knowing a cluster of doctrines. It's the heart response we want. As R. C. Sproul points out, in matters of Christian faith, the heart has primacy. God looks on the heart. He doesn't count how many things you know about him; he wants to know that your heart is his. He's not impressed that you can list each point of the gospel clearly and in order if you have never believed it. In this way, the heart has primacy. But, as Sproul also points out, in matters of Christian faith, the *head* has primacy in the sense that there must be truth in it for

8. Ibid., 10.
9. Ibid., 86.

the heart to believe.[10] Awakening that heart response is not the task of the parent or the teacher; it's the task of the Holy Spirit. The task of parent and teacher is to provide the truth to which the heart will respond. We pile up doctrinal truth in the minds of our children, and we eagerly await the Holy Spirit who alone can cause that truth to give life. But the truth needs to be there! People can know truth intellectually and yet fail to respond to it. But can they respond to truth they *don't* know? Filling our children's minds with the words of a good catechism is one of the most effective ways to make sure our children clearly know and understand the truths of Scripture to which, we hope, their hearts will one day respond.

How to Know

- Rely on a catechism to teach clear definitions of biblical terms.
- Prepare children's hearts to respond to the truths of Scripture by making sure those truths are firmly in their minds.

WHY CATECHISM? AS EXPOSITION AND APPLICATION OF GOD'S LAW

And, speaking of heart response, another benefit of using the Reformed catechisms is that they provide such excellent expositions of God's law, with convicting applications included. Children are, like all of us, naturally self-righteous. I *know* what the Ten Commandments are; so, of course, I'm keeping them, right? The catechisms point out all the ways each commandment can be broken, beyond just the surface meaning of the literal words, much as Jesus said that, if we hate or despise a brother, we have not kept the commandment to not murder (Matt. 5:21–22). Both the Heidelberg Catechism and the Westminster catechisms force us, as Jesus did, to face the fact that keeping a commandment doesn't just mean I avoid what it forbids; it means that I *do* the opposite.

Here is a sample. The Heidelberg asks, in question 94, "What does the Lord require in the first commandment ['You shall have no other gods before me']?" The answer, in part:

10. R. C. Sproul, "Have You Lost Your Mind?," *The Christian Mind: 2012 National Conference*, DVD (Orlando: Ligonier, 2012).

That I rightly know the only true God,
>trust him alone,
>and look to God for every good thing
>>humbly and patiently,
>and love, fear, and honor God
>>with all my heart.
In short,
>that I give up anything
>rather than go against God's will in any way.[11]

The catechism will not allow us to be content with our performance as long as we're not bowing to a statue. The standard rises much higher than that. It is hopelessly high—as God's standard is hopelessly high—so that we can't go on thinking we're meeting that standard. When we work through the studies of the Ten Commandments found in either the Heidelberg or the Westminster with our children, we will help them to see their own hearts and, hopefully, their need of a Savior.

Parents will find these studies in God's law helpful also in day-to-day parenting, since such a big part of daily parenting is correcting sinful behavior and training in godly behavior. Learning the Ten Commandments and what they mean as the catechisms explain them will help you hold up God's standard for your children.

How to Know

- Rely on a catechism for excellent exposition of the Ten Commandments' applications.

A FEW BASIC HOW-TO IDEAS

Church and home can work together on teaching a catechism, and that would be the most effective way to go about it. After families have worked at home through the week on learning a catechism answer, the pastor could ask the catechism question on Sunday morning, for

---

11. Faith Alive Christian Resources, *The Heidelberg Catechism: 450th Anniversary Edition* (Faith Alive Christian Resources, 2013), 55.

all who know it to answer back (with an option for reading from the bulletin for those who haven't learned it well enough to say it from memory). After ten weeks or so, there could be a special time for the pastor to read through the questions learned most recently, having children take turns reciting the answers. A certificate for each child who has memorized the answers would be a nice touch. However, something is always better than nothing. If you're a church teaching a catechism with less help from parents than you'd like, if you're a parent teaching catechism without reinforcement from your church, or if church and home are working together, here are some ideas to enhance your teaching.

Memorization is one of the easiest things the brain does—even though, the older we get, the less true that seems to be. Children memorize easily. They still need drill, however. Below are some fun ways to memorize and drill catechism answers (or Bible verses, for that matter).

Younger children do well with a chant or a tune or some rhythmic way of reciting the words. If you can set the words to a familiar tune—or to a new, simple one—or develop a chant or clapping pattern to go with the words, memorizing will suddenly become easier for your younger children.

Children, especially in groups, enjoy reciting in response to specific "personal" questions, such as:

> "Recite the answer, if you like dogs better than horses."
> ". . . if you would rather skate than swim."
> ". . . if you like math better than reading."
> ". . . if you had cereal for breakfast."
> ". . . if you've ever gone camping."
> ". . . if you're wearing blue."

Another effective way to memorize, especially a new catechism answer, is by reading through the answer, written on a whiteboard (or viewed on a computer screen) two or three times, then erasing a couple of words at a time and repeating it each time until the whole answer is gone, and you're still saying it with no written words to lean on.

Teach for meaning. Avoid having children memorize words without understanding their meanings. There are helps available, both for family situations[12] and for classes.[13] You can help children think through the meaning of what they're memorizing by holding up the various pieces of the statement for closer examination. For instance:

> Q. 86. What is faith in Jesus Christ?
> A. Faith in Jesus Christ is a saving grace, by which we receive and rest on him alone for salvation, as he is offered to us in the gospel.

- What is faith in Jesus Christ? Draw a box around one noun. ("grace")
- What kind of a grace is it? Draw an arrow from that word to "grace." ("saving")
- What two things do we do by faith? Circle two words. ("receive"; "rest")
- What do we receive? Draw an arrow to it. ("him")
- What do we rest on? Draw an arrow to it. ("him")
- Who is "him"? Draw an arrow from "him" to his name. ("Jesus Christ")
- What do we receive him for? Underline it once. ("salvation")
- What do we rest on him for? Underline it once. ("salvation")
- What else do we receive for salvation? Put a box around it.
- What else do we rest on? Put a box around it. (Nothing, of course, so children would box the word "alone.")
- What is offered to us? Circle it. ("he")

---

12. I have written two books of short, daily devotional readings based on catechism answers and including Bible texts showing where the truth is found in the Bible: *Training Hearts, Teaching Minds: Family Devotions Based on the Shorter Catechism* (Phillipsburg, NJ: P&R Publishing, 2000) and *Comforting Hearts, Teaching Minds: Family Devotions Based on the Heidelberg Catechism* (Phillipsburg, NJ: P&R Publishing, 2013). I wrote these with children of kindergarten age and older in mind.

13. G. I. Williamson, *The Westminster Shorter Catechism for Study Classes* (Phillipsburg, NJ: P&R Publishing, 2003). I would recommend this book for children in middle school or older.

- Who is "he"? Draw an arrow back to who he is. (Jesus Christ)
- Where is Jesus Christ offered to us? Put a box around it. ("in the gospel")

One final thing to keep in mind: while we teach for meaning, we don't *only* teach what children can understand, just as pastors don't only teach and preach what every adult in their audience can understand. Everyone, no matter the age in years, is at a different place, both intellectually and spiritually, concerning what they can understand. Better to ask our children to reach higher than to keep things "easy," where there will be no need to stretch in either their intellectual or their spiritual comprehension. As we provide teaching that stretches, we wait on the Holy Spirit to give understanding in his time for each of our students. We pray as we teach, asking God to ignite the doctrinal kindling we have carefully stacked.

How to Know

- Recognize and affirm children's accomplishments in memorizing catechism answers.
- With young children, set catechism answers to chants, rhythm, or familiar tunes.
- Find fun ways to drill questions and answers.
- Teach for meaning, providing explanations of answers and definitions of words.
- Show children the source of the catechism's truths by reading relevant passages of Scripture together.
- Teach so that children have to be always stretching themselves.

14

Additional Help

This book neglects several very important things. Pertaining to the raising of children who will be disciples of the Lord Jesus, this book neglects everything *except* faithful teaching of truth to their minds. But as every parent knows, there is much more to discipling children than *just* filling minds with truth. While this book stresses the importance of teaching Bible and Christian doctrine to your children, it doesn't tell you what the whole of the Bible's content is, and neither does it provide a comprehensive survey of Christianity's essential truths. While this book gives some basic topics that should be taught to children and a few hints on how to teach them, it doesn't give you material you could actually read or study with them. This last short chapter seeks to address those neglected areas by suggesting resources you may find helpful. (An important disclaimer: Just because a book ends up in this little chapter of resources does not mean that I wholeheartedly agree with every single point it makes. It only means that, overall, I believe it to be a helpful book. Not only that, but some of the resources I list I have not read myself. In those cases, I am relying on the suggestions of people whose theology and whose parenting I trust.)

RESOURCES FOR ADULT STUDY

Some parents will respond to this book's call for thorough teaching of Bible content and Christian doctrine with the cry, "But I don't know these things myself. I didn't grow up learning these things; how can I teach them to my children?" It's never too late to learn! You will find your own faith enriched and your soul rising in worship as you begin to dig into the Bible and into Christian theology yourself. The added bonus will come in the treasure trove of riches you will then be able to share with your children. There are many excellent resources available, and a trusted pastor or elder can provide you with suggestions as to what would be helpful for you. Tell him what you would like to know more about and what level of depth you need, then ask what he recommends. Below I list a few of my favorites. There are many others, but this can get you started.

For getting to know the big picture of the Bible as well as the details of its sixty-six books, there's nothing like digging into the Bible itself. Get recommendations from people you trust for a good study Bible, because it will give background and context information for each book of the Bible, along with an outline of each book to get you started and notes throughout the text providing insightful explanations. I recommend *The ESV Study Bible*, *The Reformation Study Bible*, and *The Literary Study Bible*. A missionary friend of mine, who teaches in a Bible college, said, after reading through *The ESV Study Bible* in a year, that it was as good as taking college level Old Testament and New Testament survey classes.

For big picture/overview books, I recommend D. A. Carson's *The God Who Is There: Finding Your Place in God's Story* (Baker). This takes you through the big story of the entire Bible in fourteen chapters. While new Christians can use it to get the "lay of the land" of the Bible's plotline and themes, more mature Christians will also find plenty of insights they had not considered before, and, time and again, both types of believers will find themselves pausing to worship. This book is also available as a series of lectures in a free video file on thegospelcoalition.org.

A similar big-picture resource, but with a focus on each separate book in the Bible, is *How To Read the Bible Book by Book: A Guided Tour* by Gordon Fee and Douglas Stuart (Zondervan). As they promise in their title, these authors supply an introduction to every book in the Bible, telling the reader what he or she needs to know in terms of background for it to make sense, demonstrating where and how it fits into the Bible's big story, and pointing out details to watch for along the way as the book is read.

You can approach learning the Bible's big story from a different angle with O. Palmer Robertson's *Understanding the Land of the Bible: A Biblical-Theological Guide*. Biblical theology is the study of God's truth in the order in which it was revealed, little by little, through the centuries, from creation and the first promise of a Messiah in the garden of Eden down through the apostles' writings after Jesus' resurrection and ascension. Dr. Robertson takes his readers on a tour of the relatively small geographical area in which Bible history took place, pointing out the significant events that occurred at different times in each important location. It's a small, readable book that gives fascinating insight into how times and places in Bible history fit together.

Good commentaries on specific books of the Bible can help you learn more detail about each of those books. There are many available, though not all are equally sound or equally rich in content. Here, recommendations from someone you trust will again prove invaluable. One idea would be to browse the Internet for commentaries on a book of the Bible you'd like to know better, then jot down authors' names and ask a well-read Christian whose theology you trust to tell you which names he/she knows.

As far as learning essential doctrines of the Christian faith, a logical place to start would be with the great Protestant catechisms, my two favorite being the Westminster Shorter Catechism and the Heidelberg Catechism. Both have modern English editions, which I recommend. The whole purpose behind writing the catechisms was to provide instruction for new or young believers in those convictions that must be held for a Christian faith that is in line with the Bible's teaching. A volume that gives short, very readable, very devotional commentary on the Heidelberg (itself very devotional) is Kevin DeYoung's *The Good News We Almost Forgot: Rediscovering the Gospel in a Sixteenth-Century Catechism* (Moody). Another option for adult reading is Sam Waldron's *A Modern Exposition of the 1689 Baptist Confession* (EP Books).

A Concise Theology by J.I. Packer (Tyndale House) is just as concise as it promises, still managing to explain the basics of just under a hundred key Christian beliefs, each one laid out in two pages (two and a half at the most), and including numerous Scripture references for each concept. For an in-depth look at "theology proper" (the doctrines of God), I recommend two classics: *Knowing God*, also by Packer (IVP), and *The Attributes of God* by A. W. Pink (Sovereign Grace Publishers).

Bigger books that introduce the reader to Christianity's basics are Michael Scott Horton's *The Christian Faith: A Systematic Theology for Pilgrims on the Way* (Zondervan) and R.C. Sproul's *Everyone's a Theologian: An Introduction to Systematic Theology* (Reformation Trust). For that matter, anything put out by Ligonier (a vehicle for Dr. Sproul's teaching ministry) will prove to be excellent, in terms of being both doctrinally sound and clearly, understandably communicated. Ligonier's whole purpose for existing has always been to educate ordinary Christians; on offer are books, DVDs, CDs, and online resources galore. It's worth browsing Ligonier's website at Ligonier.org.

RESOURCES TO PREPARE ADULTS TO TEACH CHILDREN

A classic for getting an overview of the Bible through its stories is the four-volume *Promise and Deliverance* by S. G. DeGraaf (Paideia Press/Reformational Publishing Project). This was written as a resource for children's teachers. It takes teachers through the Bible's stories, Genesis through Revelation, showing how they all revolve around God's covenantal promises.

Another resource for teachers is the more recent (and more concise) *The Bible Story Handbook: A Resource for Studying 175 Stories from the Bible* by John Walton and Kim Walton (Crossway). This book is worth the cost simply for the introduction, which makes an excellent case for teaching the Bible so children will know who God is, without obsessing over application right here and now, and without making moral points based on the human characters' behavior. For each of the 175 stories included in the book, the authors give a Lesson Focus (which is always what God is doing in the story), applications (always based on the truth about God seen in the story), information on the story's context, its background, interpretational issues, and mistakes to avoid.

Show Them Jesus: Teaching the Gospel to Kids by Jack Klumpenhower (New Growth Press) works hard to communicate to teachers especially (but parents are teachers too) the reason for, and the how-tos of, teaching Bible stories in such a way that we present the person and the work of Christ to the children we teach. This is highly readable and full of good examples showing how it's done.

RESOURCES FOR TEACHING CHILDREN

When I worked as a director of children's ministries for a church and while I was raising my own children, there was very little available in the way of Bible storybooks that weren't either moralistic or child-centered in their approach (see chapter 12). There are several good books for children available now that I am happy to recommend for reading to or with children. Here is a list of some of them:

The Big Picture Story Bible by David Helm (Crossway). This gives a short, simplified overview of the Bible's main story, centered on the concept of "God's people in God's place under God's rule."[1] Twenty-six very short stories loaded with beautiful, full-page illustrations by Gail Schoonmaker give a succinct overview of the story of God keeping all his promises to have a people who would be his people. The simple vocabulary, short stories, and colorful illustrations make this book ideal for use with young children through early grade school.

Often, what is most popular as a children's Bible storybook is *not* something I would want to recommend. At the moment, however, that is not the case, and the one that sells the best is really a very good Bible storybook. It is Sally Lloyd-Jones's *The Jesus Storybook Bible: Every Story Whispers his Name* (Zondervan). Forty-four stories, again with beautiful illustrations, this time by Jago, come back, every time, to Jesus and the salvation he would bring (Old Testament stories) or has brought (New Testament stories). This book is suitable for the next age up after *The Big Picture Story Bible*—I'd say kindergarten through third grade.

For the next age up (third through sixth grade): *Grandpa's Box: Retelling the Biblical Story of Redemption* (P&R) by Starr Meade with

1. David Helm, *The Big Picture Story Bible* (Wheaton, IL: Crossway, 2004), 13.

black and white illustrations by Bruce van Patter. A grandfather seizes every occasion to tell "war" stories to his grandchildren, in this case the war between God, who purposed to have a people for himself, and Satan, who opposed him every step of the way. Beginning in Genesis and moving up to the birth of Christ, Grandpa tells stories of God's promises of a Savior and the many potential obstacles to his coming, then goes on to tell of the advance of that Savior's kingdom through the New Testament stories, ending at the end—Revelation. Forty-four chapters.

Mighty Acts of God: A Family Bible Story Book by Starr Meade (Crossway) retells ninety Bible stories, Genesis through Revelation, emphasizing in child-appropriate vocabulary what the story teaches about God and about important doctrinal concepts. Each of the ninety stories is followed by brief suggestions for further discussion and for application. Stories are intended for third through sixth graders and include color illustrations by Tim O'Connor. *Wondrous Works of God: A Family Bible Story Book* is a second volume, with all the same features, beginning again in Genesis and moving through Revelation, but with ninety completely different stories.

Marty Machowski has written three books for use by parents with their children: *Long Story Short: Ten-Minute Devotions to Draw Your Family to God*; *Old Story New: Ten-Minute Devotions to Draw Your Family to God*; and *The Gospel Story Bible: Discovering Jesus in the Old and New Testaments* (all New Growth Press). The first two (*Long Story Short* and *Old Story New*) don't retell Bible stories; instead, they provide Bible references to look up and read aloud from the Bible. Short sections ("Think About It," "Talk About It," and "Pray About It") follow. *Long Story Short* takes a family through the Old Testament and *Old Story New* picks up the Bible's story beginning with the New Testament. (My opinion is that you should not take the "ten-minute devotions" claim in the title too seriously. While you could surely do the reading aloud in ten minutes, the point is to discuss and pray as well, and I don't believe you could fit all that's provided into ten minutes, especially if you have more than one child!) *The Gospel Story Bible* retells Bible stories for children, with Jesus as the central focus of them all, and with illustrations.

Older students (middle school and older) can dig into serious Bible study for themselves, on their own or with parents studying alongside, with the four-volume set *The Most Important Thing You'll Ever Study: A Survey of the Bible* by Starr Meade (Crossway). This work is a set of four workbooks (two Old Testament, two New Testament) and a fifth booklet that is the answer key. The student will learn the background of each book in the Bible and will be led through that book's highlights through references to look up and read with questions to answer about the passage. The emphasis is on how all the books fit together into one whole, and what we see about God and his plan of redemption throughout. An optional plan to read through the entire Bible is provided along with the references for specific "highlight" passages in each Bible book. This survey came from a Bible class for junior high and early high school students I taught and is intended to take at least two, maybe three, years to complete.

Books for children that focus on particular topics are *Leading Little Ones to God* by Marian Schoolland (Eerdmans) and the Making Him Known series from Next Generation Resources: *God's Names, God's Promise, God's Providence, God's Wisdom, God's Battle,* and *God's Word* (P&R). Bible stories illustrate the concepts and each story gives suggested activities.

Marvelous music resources for children can be found at songsfor saplings.com. You may listen to many of the songs online. They are simple, highly singable songs whose lyrics are catechism questions and answers with related Bible verses. Careful, though: Songs for Saplings uses The New City Catechism, a contemporary catechism drawing from the older Reformed versions. If you're working hard with your children to memorize one of the older, classic catechisms, the different arrangement of questions and answers could be confusing.

RESOURCES FOR THE REST OF PARENTING

There is a great deal more to raising children to be followers of Christ than teaching them the content of the Bible and of the Christian faith. The following resources give excellent help in some of the other important areas of Christian parenting.

Susan Hunt provides something of a theology of discipling children in *Heirs of the Covenant: Leaving a Legacy of Faith for the Next Generation* (Crossway). She gives the biblical basis for teaching children the truth of God's Word in the context of the covenant God has made with his people. Hunt gives equal emphasis to the content our children should learn and the context in which they should be learning it—the covenant community, both their own families and the larger household of God

Shepherding a Child's Heart (Shepherd Press) by Tedd Tripp has become a best seller, and happily so. Tripp demonstrates that faithful discipline is far more than simply controlling children's behavior. God and the gospel aim at the heart; heart change is what we as parents must seek, too. The book is loaded with practical advice on using times of discipline to shepherd your child's heart, seeking genuine repentance and heart change. This material is available as a curriculum or simply as a book. Later, Tripp coauthored *Instructing a Child's Heart* (Shepherd Press) with his wife, Margy. This book looks at specific areas of daily life as it's lived with growing children, guiding parents in teaching children to see from the Bible's perspective.

Give Them Grace: Dazzling Your Kids with the Love of Jesus by Elyse Fitzpatrick and Jessica Thompson (Crossway) sounds a similar note. Never be content with requiring good behavior from children as you provide the needed correction that parenting requires. We don't want them to come to believe themselves capable of works righteousness. Always lead them through correction back to the gospel and the free grace of God in Christ.

Paul David Tripp, Tedd's brother, focuses on parenting teenagers in an excellent book *Age of Opportunity: A Biblical Guide to Parenting Teens* (P&R).

We would all love to see our children not only *not* bicker, tattle, and tease, but actually enjoy one another. A set of siblings, Sarah, Stephen, and Grace Mally, have written *Making Brothers and Sisters Best Friends* (Forefathers, Inc.) to show us how it's done.

Training our children in worship is one of the most important things we will ever do. Jason Helopoulos has written an excellent, encouraging, guilt-free (and short!) book on leading families in daily (or, at least, regular) times of worship at home: *A Neglected Grace: Family Worship in the Christian Home* (Christian Focus). Noël Piper, in *Treasuring God in Our Traditions*

(Crossway), guides parents in building their family traditions in such a way that God is honored and loved in them. An appendix at the end, "The Family Together in God's Presence," cowritten with her husband, John Piper, explains the reasons for taking children into the worship service with you, as opposed to leaving them in a program for children. The Pipers provide excellent, practical advice on how to make this work and on how to make it something children profit and grow from. Robbie Castleman provides even more help in this area with an entire book entitled *Parenting in the Pew: Guiding Your Children into the Joy of Worship* (IVP).

There is plenty in every aspect of parenting to induce guilt. In parenting, as in everything we do since the fall and until Christ returns, we continue to be sinners. We will neglect more things that we should have done than we can ever count. We will do and say all sorts of things we should never have done or said. Here, as in every aspect of life, we rejoice to know that God deals with us, always, on the basis of his grace, never on the basis of what we deserve. When he saves our children or anyone else, he always does it because he is gracious, never because someone—whether a child or his parents—has merited it.

Nor are there guarantees that our diligence will always produce the results we long for. In every area of parenting or teaching children, our task is to seek to be faithful to what God calls us to do—repenting when we fail and realizing that we will fail often, and seeking God's help for the same things, over and over. All the while, we ask God to work in the hearts of our children, for, even if we could parent or teach perfectly (which, of course, we cannot), our best efforts would never be enough to change the hearts of stone with which our children were born. As Samuel Rutherford wrote several times in letters to his friends: "Duties are ours, but events are the Lord's."[2] And so we parent and so we teach, rejoicing that our God is much more faithful in bringing results than we will ever be in fulfilling our duties.

2. Andrew A. Bonar, *Letters of Samuel Rutherford* (Carlisle, PA: Banner of Truth Trust, 1984), 175.

Starr Meade has over twenty-five years of experience teaching children from Christian families in church, Christian school, and homeschool classes. She served for ten years as director of the Christian education ministry for all children under twelve in a local church. She taught Latin and Bible full-time in a Christian school for eight years, working with students from third through ninth grade. She currently teaches history, English, art history, and literature classes for home-schooled teenagers. Meade's experience with a variety of ages led her to write *Give Them Truth*, as she has seen example after example of Christian students who know very little about the Bible or about the Christian faith they claim to hold.